MICHELLE-J. NOEL

CREATE THE LIFE YOU WANT

Choose your life

FINDHORN PRESS

Published in 2011 by Findhorn Press, Scotland and Quintessence Publisher, France.

ISBN 978-1-84409-552-0

A CIP record for this title is available from the British Library.

Printed and bound in the European Union

1 2 3 4 5 6 7 8 9 17 16 15 14 13 12 11

Published by

Findhorn Press
117-121 High Street,
Forres IV36 1AB,
Scotland, UK

Tel +44 (0)1309 690582
Fax +44 (0)131 777 2711
email: info@findhornpress.com
www.findhornpress.com

Quintessence Publisher
Rue de la Bastidonne
13678 Aubagne Cedex
France

Tél. (+33) 04 42 18 90 94
Fax (+33) 04 42 18 90 99
email: info@holoconcept.eu
www.editions-quintessence.com

Introduction and thanks

I arrived in the world in 1946, covered in eczema, at a time of great turmoil in my parents' lives. Forty years later I came to realise that my eczema was a physical (biological) manifestation of fear, of a sense of separation from my parents.

My brain/computer had no option but to engage with the "rejection" my mother had experienced during pregnancy and childbirth. As a consequence I spent a large part of my life seeking to be accepted and loved, to become integrated. I compensated in my struggle over my own sense of self-worth by spending long periods studying illness, firstly, and subsequently its causes.

These continuous and wide-ranging studies enabled me to meet exceptional teachers, to integrate a wonderful understanding of the universe, of mankind and its way of thinking, helping others heal and so emerge from their schema or closed model of thinking.

My real aim was to heal myself and to find my true place with my parents, present or absent.

Happiness does exist, and is within your grasp. All you have to do is want it, imagine it, decide on it, program it and have one hundred per cent belief in the power of your subconscious.

This book is for every man or woman who is convinced that happiness is only for others; for everyone lost in the labyrinth of their future, entangled in their own decisions or in a state of breakdown over past trauma. From every apparently unpleasant or dramatic situation we can, if we look, draw something useful. If we are prepared to live through the experience, then a way out (a solution) is presented to us, a path opens before us, leading us from good to better, to new adventures.

If you want to find someone in a crowd, you think exclusively of them. Your brain scans their image until, all of a sudden, you see them. If you had done the opposite and observed the crowd, you would not have found them.

Observe, think what you really want, hold your dreams and have confidence in your unequalled inner power, your subconscious brain.

I would like to thank my younger brother for helping me in a number of ways to complete this book.

I would also like to thank my teachers: John Grinder, Robert Dilts, Tony Robbins, Steven Brooks, Gilbert Altenbach, Boone Legrais, Bernard Wœstland and Maxie Maulsby for their pragmatic and elegant ways of helping others and creating solutions.

I thank my two sons: Benoît for his research and Sébastien for his help.

Above all I thank my fantastic parents for teaching me courage and responsibility by showing me the way to live one's dreams.

I dedicate this book to my grandsons Kévin and Guillaume, and to all those yet to come, that they may learn to take charge of their own destinies and make masterpieces of their lives.

I also dedicate this book to everyone who thinks they are out of luck. Luck and chance do not exist. Each individual, even the most destitute, has the inner power to turn a problem into a solution, to open new doors and to succeed in life.

My aim in this book is to initiate you into realising your dreams, not in a magical fashion, but in a real pragmatic, practical, useful and do-able way. When dream becomes reality it is not magic, but conscious or unconscious programming.

This book will become your companion; it will lead you to success.

You have only to cover its six stages to see the end of the tunnel and the sun breaking through the clouds.

CONTENTS

CONTENTS

Chapter I

A STUDY OF THE PRESENT

Current life report

I have often asked myself why so many brave people, having failed in their marriage, their job or some other undertaking and then ploughing straight back into new experiences, fall into the same behaviour patterns, meet the same types of people and tirelessly relive the same unhappy experiences. They do this in spite of displaying resources of willpower, creative visualisation or positive thinking.

Through wide reading and study I had been aware for several years of the brain's fantastic properties. I knew "how" to program a more appropriate future. But in spite of this, in many cases things didn't work out. I searched for an explanation in a number of recent studies; and when you search, you find.

One day I decided to create an internet site (I already used email successfully). I changed my access provider for a more suitable one. No sooner had I subscribed than everything, including email, stopped working. I called a computer technician who said it was quite normal for everything to stop in this way. Before doing anything else you had to uninstall the old parameters and set new ones. Of course!

This is what we have to do our own computer/brain: *uninstall* a program to enable us to install a new one.

The questions is, how?

I knew how to program, but I didn't know how to deprogram. And I needed to know there was something that needed deprogramming!

In 1997 I became aware of the work of the clinical psychologist Marc Fréchet, who died in 1998. He had worked out the cycles of memorised cells, which was exactly what I needed in order to understand fully how the brain worked. Deprogramming and reprogramming.

I understood that we quite simply reproduce the patterns of thinking, the mental processes of our parents and grandparents.

In order to become truth, each new piece of information has to pass through three stages:

- Stage one: the information is ridiculed
- Stage two: it arouses violent opposition
- Stage three: it is admitted to be self-evident

These days, to dare to say that happiness exists, to maintain that we can be the author as well as the enactor of our lives, or to say that someone with a serious illness can perhaps be cured, often provokes the first two stages simultaneously: the amused laugh and violent opposition. One is all too readily suspected of belonging to some peculiar sect.

Talking about catastrophe, strikes, incurable illness, lack of security or how badly everything is going makes you normal, suitable material for television.

Thankfully, there have always been people who believe in their dreams, believe the incredible and demonstrate that the impossible is indeed possible.

If mankind had stopped at the visible, tangible universe, the universe of the senses, we would certainly have remained stuck in a dim and distant past.

We would have been able to develop only through experimental discovery: fire, stone, the wheel, steam, petrol. Man has gone further by daring to explore inner worlds.

Here are statements made according to the logic of their times by "experts" who did not attempt to explore further:

- Harry Warner, of the famous Warner Brothers Pictures said at the time when people were starting to envisage the addition of sound to silent films: "Who the hell wants to hear actors talk?"

- In 1878, the president of the US Western Union rail company said of the telephone: "What use has this company for an electrical toy?"

- In 1899, Charles Duell, commissioner of the United States Patent and Trademark Office insisted: "Everything that can be invented has been invented."

- In 1895, Lord Kelvin, one of the most brilliant physicists of his generation, said: "Heavier-than-air flying machines are impossible!" Etc.

The more one insists on opposing the new, the more one slows down its acceptance as reality. Fortunately, throughout history there have been men and women who, through their own imaginations, have gone beyond the known to concentrate on innovation and utility.

According to Chris Morton and Ceri Louise Thomas in their book "The Mystery of the Crystal Skulls", experiments in quantum physics suggest that it is possible for the human spirit to communicate directly with inanimate objects, at least on the subatomic level. An experiment conducted in 1989 by Wayne Itano and colleagues at the National Institute of Standards and Technology in Boulder, Colorado was reported by Dr. Fred Alan Wolf in his book "The Dreaming Universe". It consisted of the researchers observing some 5,000 atoms of beryllium in a magnetic field exposed to radio waves. To help understand the experiment, Fred Alan Wolf gives the analogy of a pot of water which one observes in bringing it to the boil. The experiment confirmed that the pot of water never boils when it is under observation. The more the researchers observed the process, the longer the beryllium atoms took to "boil". According to Dr. Wolf the results of the experiment were affected the by the "observer effect". This principle, generally accepted today in quantum research, is as follows: "The more a quantum system in observed in a particular state, the higher the probability that it will remain in that state."

13

It is the observer's **intention** that counts, says Dr. Wolf. Remember that if the object or system is to remain in its original state then the observer must observe it in that state. So, if the intention of the observer is to watch the pot boiling, it will boil. This "intention" is different from simply waiting. Also, the appropriate action must take place. Experiments have shown that the working of the human mind directly affects the behaviour of subatomic particles—the quantum system. There is interaction or communication between inanimate object and the human mind. Our thoughts do have the power to influence things around us in a way that can't be explained using the laws of traditional physics. It seems that in some way the very atoms are aware that they are under observation and as a result change their state or behaviour. The phenomenon suggests that even subatomic particles have a form of 'awareness' or 'perception' of what is going on around them. Native Americans call this 'the spirit of the molecules'. This consciousness seems to extend to a form of relationship between them and human thought.

By extension, observing a thing or a system in its original state makes it very likely that it will remain in that state. On the other hand, if our intention is other and we see what we truly want the thing or system to become, we will give life to the change.

When Jules Verne imagined mobile phones or even the internet, they appeared impossible. No matter whether plane, train, your glasses, car or microwave, nothing exists which was not at some stage dreamed or imagined by someone. All these things have become reality.

When the human imagination is engaged, everything becomes possible. The earth is round, it's not at the centre of the universe and it goes round the sun. Before these laws were scientifically established, they were imagined. That's how Newton discovered the laws of gravitation, how Maxwell found electromagnetic fields, Bohr the atom and Einstein the law of relativity. The human spirit has no limit to what it can discover or create, so why not use it in everyday life?

I have written this book to show you that you can rewrite your life scenario, write a fine story, set it up and live it.

But first let's find out what's in our head and what needs deprogramming.

The performance of the human brain betters the most advanced information technology; it awaits and executes any order we give it.

Whether in terms of career, behaviour, illness or love, we reproduce familial patterns, the patterns of our parents and ancestors. How do we know?

Let's look at the salmon. After swimming thousands of mille in the ocean every wild salmon in the world returns to its birthplace to reproduce. It doesn't need a map for this fantastic feat of aquatic navigation but unrolls the inner map in its own memory hologram, causing the world outside to coincide with its inner world. When the call to reproduce comes, every salmon in the world sets out on the journey to its own source.

This aquatic migration, like all migrations, follows the unwinding of internal information, in the same way that we respond to unconscious impulses.

Detailed studies of ringed birds and their resting places before migration shows that they do not land arbitrarily but rather on the same tuft of grass (to within about 4 inch) that their parent chose in the past. Every bird finds its place. This proves that flight information is memorised by each bird in its family group. The information, passed from parent to offspring in each family group, in an unchanging manner, is a proper internal road map, memorised and faithfully reused by each successive generation when the individual replays the tape.

It's the same for the salmon, except that their lesson is aquatic rather than aerial.

We, too, make exact reproductions of our parents' maps, brain to brain. But for us, unlike fish or birds, there is the opportunity, if we can become aware of it, to change the map.

It would be wrong to think that all salmon are the same any more than all humans are the same. Salmon, like humans, vary according to their continent of origin. American salmon are not the same as

European salmon and within Europe salmon vary according to country—Norwegian, Scottish, Irish all have their own characteristics. The variation extends to region: Highland Scottish salmon differ from Lowland Scottish salmon; and even with a region, salmon will vary from place to place. Each salmon, male or female, will return to its own place, it's own piece of territory.

If we take eggs from Highland Scottish salmon immediately after they have been laid and transport them to a gravel pit at the source of the Loire, with all the necessary conditions for their survival, they will develop there, then head down the Loire to the sea. Where will they return after seven years—the Scottish Highlands or the Loire?

They will return to the place where they came into the world, in this case the Loire. In this way the ancient, ancestral programme of the salmon can be changed.

From this we conclude that a salmon's eventful migration is simply invariable and unconscious obedience to unknown territorial programming conditions. What connection does this have to human beings? We reproduce unconscious programming in relation to preceding generations. It really is not our fault, nor the fault of our ancestors, if we do not succeed in certain areas of life. These are memories which go round and round.

It is reassuring to think that things have some sense to them. A life, a way of behaving, an illness devoid of meaning would seem unjust. Why are there beautiful people and ugly people, people who are ill and others in good health? It is an illusion to think that things in this beautiful universe are unjust.

Memorised cycles

Voltaire said something extraordinary: "Knowledge is freedom".

So don't launch into an endless round of therapy because, from the moment you become aware of your memories, or just from the moment you become aware that you are reproducing a set response pattern, the programme breaks, like a wiped tape. Of course you have to know what conditioning you want or need to change.

Think of the brain like this:

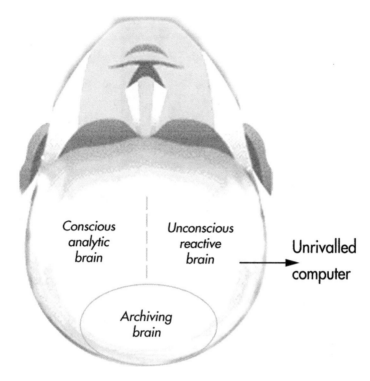

Conscious
analytic
brain

Unconscious
reactive
brain

Unrivalled
computer

Archiving
brain

Person seen from above

What is our conscious brain and what does it do? It thinks, reasons, calculates, it wants this and it doesn't want that. Consciously, we want to direct our life and think we are being logical. But just look at an iceberg: from the surface the reality we see is true, yet untrue. We see only the part which is above water, which may be very small in relation to the submerged part we cannot see. The same applies to everything we observe in our lives: what we see as true is often a completely false reality.

John Grinder, teacher of linguistics at the University of California, Santa Cruz and co-creator of Neuro-Linguistic Programming (NLP), was familiar with the work of Alfred Korzybski, father of general semantics.

So NLP was enriched with the famous slogan "The map is not the territory", which is to say that everything we perceive consciously, what we see and hear in every aspect of our life, is a reality particular to us and only one way of perceiving among many, one person or one thing or one place.

Jean Guitton said: "Nothing is real, we are at the heart of an illusion which spreads a whole succession of appearances and illusions round us, which we take for reality. We live in a perpetual state of hallucination."

Everything we are aware of is of the here and now. Of course one can consciously recollect details or elements of our earlier life. But there remains everything we are not conscious of, skills learned or acquired: walking, taking things in our hands, writing which has become automatic… All our resources, learned skills, our expertise are in our unconscious mind. We are unaware of the fact that when we consciously have a specific wish, our unconscious mind takes charge and makes it happen. We know how to make simple things happen, that's to say we let them happen because we are totally unaware of the process. On the other hand, when it's a wish you judge to be important and you want to find a solution consciously, that's when difficulties appear. The conscious mind is not necessarily fully operational or of sound judgement; it exerts considerable influence on your unconscious by way of emotions and negative beliefs.

What is our unconscious mind and how does it operate? It is in fact our best friend, the informed observer of our consciousness. It doesn't think, reason or judge and is unaware of conscious logic, possessing its own. It is in a position to intervene when we ask it to and it possesses all the necessary resources and the potential to bring about large-scale change. But the conscious mind rebels and erects barriers. Our unconscious mind can process 30 billion bits of information per second. The human nervous system contains about 28 billion neurones. Without neurones our nervous system would be unable to interpret the information we receive from our senses, transmit it to the brain and carry out the latter's instructions. Each neurone is a standalone mini-computer. Neurones act autonomously, but can also communicate with other neurones through simultaneous resonance or through an impressive network of nerve fibres, 99 420 miles long. The brain can deal with information in an astonishing manner. The reaction of a neurone can spread to hundreds of thousands of other neurones in less than 20 milliseconds, about a tenth of the time it takes to blink.

The brain/calculator can deal with several things at once. While watching a film on television you can be thinking what you will eat presently or what you have done that evening.

The brain can recognise someone in the street in less than a second. It can reach this speed because, unlike a computer which operates stage by stage, its billions of neurones can all attack the same problem at once. In addition, your brain operates in space and time.

We possess the most incredible computer on the planet, so why don't we always succeed in what we do or achieve our goals? The answer, sadly, is because no one tells us how to use it.

I'm going to teach you how to use it in the chapter called "Creating the life you want".

As well as the conscious and subconscious areas of the brain we also have an archiving brain that stores our memories. (Clearly we are unaware of this archive.)

Everything starts at conception. At the point at which the father's spermatozoon meets the mother's ovum the child has no consciousness; everything takes place from command centre to command centre, from brain to brain. How do we know?

I quote Dr. Brosse: "A Soviet researcher, the astronomer Kozyrev, detected, in relation to some telepathic experiments, an unknown energy, recorded in the form of curves and running parallel to known mechanical and chemical effects. This energy did not move in luminous waves and manifested **everywhere at the same time**. Modifying the properties of a fragment showed up everywhere at once. It is omnipresent and links us to others just as it links everything in the universe. It has a number of properties which can be studied in the laboratory. **It's density is greater near the recipient of the thought than it is near the author.** This explains how the thought is transmitted instantly, with little regard to distance, even considerable distances. The density of the energy is affected by thought and its intrinsic quality: "the density of poetry is different from that of mathematics".

There are undoubtedly people who are aware of this phenomenon and make use of it. We should be equally aware of it. I quote Bernard Wœstland on the matter: "When you have a thought which is very strong, intense, deep, it is borrowing from the invisible grid which surrounds us and will impact other people." This scientific discovery enables us to understand the words of Christ: "But I say to you that everyone who looks at a woman with lustful intent has already committed adultery with her in his heart." Matthew 5:27.

Thinking about a person can greatly disturb them.

All minds in a family group—and in the universe—are connected. We are not surrounded by empty space. We are joined together by billions of force fields (like billions of strands of spaghetti, if we were able to see what goes on around us). Consider the following metaphor: a physical chemist somewhere in the world discovers a chemical formula. A physical chemist in Paris, interested in the same area, watching some programme or other, will know the formula.

You must have noticed that a three-year old child can operate a video recorder and turn on the television. He didn't learn this for himself; he acquired the knowledge from his parents.

The experiments showing that all brains are linked one to the other were carried out in a variety of ways, for example using mice. At the end of the second world war the Russians carried out the most advanced work on the brain's potential. The results of the following experiment in Siberia was revealed thirty years later.

A biologist in a Russian laboratory had a mouse which gave birth to seven babies. He then had the idea of taking the babies, unweaned, and giving them to the commander of a Russian nuclear submarine that was about to leave on a month's underwater mission to the Pacific. The two synchronized their watches. The commander agreed to put the baby mice, singly or severally, at repeated times of his choosing, in the torpedo tube and fire them into the water (where they would of course die). During the same period the biologist would attach electrodes to the mother mouse in the laboratory in order to have a continuous scan of her brain. He even arranged emergency electrical backup in case of power failure. The scientist had no idea of the exact moment when the submariner would fire the baby mice into the water.

The seven mice were ejected at exact dates and times, different for each one. On return to base the submarine commander forwarded this data to the scientist, who compared it with his hourly printout of the mother's scan. Seven spikes (peaks of intensity) were noted at the exact times when the seven mice died, evidence of the existence of specialist waves linking brain to brain, particularly between a mother and her offspring.

This communication can also be found between the members of a herd of elephants. The elephants have a method of finding a lost calf. They all do a large circular dance. At a given moment they additionally do a 360° turn on themselves. If the adults' foreheads are in a line directly opposite the calf's, the special "S" waves, separate from known brain waves, are emitted and received. All they have to do then is to walk in that direction and find the calf.

This can also be noted in plants. The experiment has been performed using geraniums—a mother plant with 11 babies placed round her. All were well watered and fed. When a baby geranium was sprayed with toxic water and died, the other young did not react. When the mother was treated in this way, the 11 baby geraniums, healthy and supplied with spring water and fertilizer, all died too.

Dr. Thérèse Brosse's experiments on the reaction of plants to human thought also reinforce the idea that everything works from brain to brain.

Experiments carried out in France and England show the psychic influence that can be exerted on growth and germination. Wheat, parsley and red flax have all been the subject of unusual experiments. A quarter of an hour's thought per day for a week was sufficient to produce a result; going on longer turned out to be a waste of time. Seeds, separated into two groups, were sown in the same pot, identical distances apart one from another in each group. The seeds were subjected to two different treatments: one activating development, the other slowing it down. Without ever telling this team what he was doing the experimenter created a fine mental image of what he wanted to achieve with the seeds he cherished; in the same way he imagined the opposite group of seeds not growing. He also talked to his subjects in opposing affective terms. On the one hand "You are beautiful, you please me, you will grow"; on the other "You are not beautiful, you are thin, you do not please me, you will not grow". Sometimes physical effort, in thought form, was associated with the process, for example going uphill on a bicycle linked to the thought of the plant's growth. The result was fine plants on one side and scrawny ones on the other.

We could recount a number of experiments by researchers interested in this question. Cleve Backster showed plants' reaction to suffering by plunging shrimps into boiling water next to one. When he presented shrimps that were already dead the plant showed no reaction; when the shrimps were alive the electrical measuring device attached to the plant showed a surge as the plant reacted to the shrimps' suffering. Backster discovered that fruit, vegetables, moulds, blood and yeast displayed the same sensitivity to the distress of another life.

At the moment of conception, when sperm meets egg, from brain to brain, the infant memorises the following in its archives:

- **The climate** at conception—the life of the age: war, peace, the parents' situation, living conditions, family relations, the general atmosphere;
- **The plans** of the parents (professional, romantic or for the child itself);
- **Conflict**—everything that annoys me and that I cannot resolve.

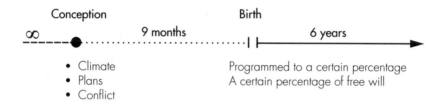

For nine months the child lives in its mother's belly, in the climate, the plans and the conflicts of its parents. When it arrives in the world it is programmed to a greater degree than it has free will and this continues until it is six years old (a child needs contact with its mother until the age of six). From conception to six the child memorises the climate, plans and conflicts of its family, and throughout its life it will translate their meaning.

You might arrive in the world with a heavy programme to bear, like a big suitcase to carry. There's no question of putting it down because we are formed by our past and cannot ignore those who went before us. It took an enormous number of people to get us where we are today. On the other hand it will be up to us to change the content, renew things, do the washing, so increasing the degree of free-will. Our problem in life is simply that we are not aware of this creative work which has to be done.

Julia was a pretty woman of 45, elegant and intelligent. She had been married three times and had two sons from her first marriage. Her three husbands had been identical, all highly unfaithful and she had suffered each time before deciding to separate. She had succeeded in her professional life, which had blossomed while her private life, in spite of two fine children whom she loved, remained an emotional desert, suffering failure after failure. Later we will see that failure does not exist, it is merely an outcome.

What had happened to her, whether at conception, during the nine months' gestation, or during birth?

Questioning her 75 year old mother Joséphine about her parents' life when she, Julia was conceived, she found that the fairytale she had imagined had in fact been a tragedy.

Josephine told her that when she was three months pregnant her mother-in-law (Julia's paternal grandmother) came to see her and said "Joséphine, do something, your husband is at the seaside flirting with a young woman." Her world turned suddenly upside down, for she loved her husband very much. Two minutes earlier she had been happy, now her whole pregnancy was disrupted by questions she couldn't answer; she felt betrayed.

Julia asked her mother "so what did you do?" "Nothing," she replied, "I wanted to separate from your father, but I couldn't, I already had your sister and I was pregnant."

This was the first time Julia heard the word "separate". She had experienced infidelity with successive husbands, and betrayal, but she had never understood the concept of "separation". She herself had decided three times to separate from her unfaithful husbands, three times she had left for a new and she hoped better life. Julia understood the following:

- The climate of the time: unfaithfulness
- Her parents' plans: to separate
- The conflict: betrayal

What fine programming. At the moment of her birth her father was courting another woman and her mother knew it, without knowing who it was.

Looked at like this it was not the fault of her husbands if Julia was deceived; we might say it was the fault of her programming.

In fact she would discover it was no one's fault. "Unconscious atoms hooked together". Her subconscious mind had attracted to her those who corresponded to that memory.

She could change the mental map and make new choices. All she had to do was to become aware of it in order to move on; this was part of her story, part of the role she had to play in order to promote her family group and create a new life.

Something particularly interesting in the work of Marc Fréchet, French psychologist, is the awareness with which we reproduce programmes. What is the point? Undoubtedly to cancel them, not to complain endlessly about them. Sometimes we go through life on automatic pilot, thinking that we inevitably have no luck, but it's not true. Memorised cycles can simply awaken us from our torpor and remove the guilt associated with our negative behaviour. And so we can stop thinking or acting in a particular, familiar way; for thing will keep on happening until the day we learn to say "stop".

Whether it is memorised cycles, the study of genealogy or simple awareness on our part, the principle involved is one of awakening. Many people prefer to think that others are responsible for their problems, that they are what they are because of their family background! This is true and untrue at the same time.

It's up to us to change certain aspects of ourselves which we reproduce so effectively even though they belong to other men and women of our clan. Starting from a present with which you are dissatisfied, fix on objectives and new route maps which will enable you to reach the state you desire. I have met many men and women who ask what they were put on this earth to do. You came here to evolve, to promote your family group and to make your life a masterpiece.

When you live through a drama or a situation which does not suit you, you are presented with two paths you can follow, like your two arms: the left arm is the way of problems, the right arm the way of solutions. You cannot travel both routes simultaneously. You have an option. Many people go through life thinking they have no choice other than the one they are living, which is to say the problem. But as soon as you have an intention, a precise objective, and your unconscious brain is ready to help you find solutions and go off in other directions, then a multitude of choices are available to you.

If you choose the left path, the problem path, I won't be with you; you won't arrive anywhere, or if you do it will be in a cul-de-sac. On the right-hand path, the path of solutions, the first thing I suggest is you discover the useful, positive function of everything that happens to you. For there is a point, or maybe several. Nothing is by chance.

That is why I have devoted at paragraph at the end of the book to synchronicity, to help you better interpret events. On the other hand there is really nothing to interpret, because the message is always explicitly contained in the event. So don't interpret the synchronicities, write the text of your adventure in your own words and the message will reveal itself to you (see the chapter on "Synchronicity").

Let's go back to Voltaire's maxim "Knowledge is freedom". Is it specific knowledge of our personal history that can free us, or simply an understanding that we do reproduce historic mental maps, and that what happens to us is neither our fault nor the fault of our forebears, who didn't do what they did "on purpose" to "annoy" us? As soon as the information reaches our consciousness (recovering the real weight of things), the tape in our subconscious stops. But what information?

You can turn into Inspector Colombo if you want to and set out to discover the mood or climate that appertained the day of your conception, and your parents' plans and conflicts. This way is often difficult. Adopted children will be frustrated not to have any information at all, while the twelfth or seventeenth child of a large family will be unlikely to make head or tail of it. If your parents have died you will think "I've had it, no information for me." But there is a better way.

Or you can—and this is the more interesting route—choose to take stock of your life. "What's not working?" You can realise that these are not your mental maps and decide, by creating the right emotion, to get rid of them. How do you wipe the tape clean? By recording something else onto it. You can you know.

Take a general problem, a health issue for example. What do you believe about it? Often it's an involuntary rehearsal of scenarios repeated down the generations: one's behaviour in given situations; illnesses which recur from generation to generation; things that are triggered when one wishes they wouldn't be; or regularly falling flat on your face in some supposedly well-rehearsed area of your life.

Or you can simply leave the current problem behind. Find the belief that you can do so.

Subsequently you can go back into your past and discover the moment, the very first time you set it up. How? Associate yourself with the problem, which is to say talk to yourself about your concern, express it, live it, resent it, clench your fist at the height of your emotion. Close your eyes and ask your subconscious mind quietly to go back into your far past, to the very first occasion on which you were aware of the feeling which you have just experienced and expressed. Your unconscious will take you to the first time you put in place your family's mental maps. The child you were then (your younger self) evaluated the situation through its contemporary filters, its beliefs, and then took an unconscious decision about the behaviour to adopt. It's this first-time decision, taken according to your subconscious programming, which has determined your current state.

A first stage is to look at the childhood part of yourself, at the circumstances of the decision from the standpoint of that time and to decide what you think is no longer useful, as well perhaps as considering whether the decision you took was the only possible option. Your parents themselves acted in terms of their own unconscious realities. Rehabilitating them might free your life. Look for their positive intent rather than criticising them, because your childish realities are only interpretations of true reality. Bring your "inner child" to believe something different about this experience, something more appropriate, more positive, entirely beneficial. And push it towards putting a new decision in place, one with a positive influence for your life today and which you can allow to succeed. Find the positive intent of the parents and others involved, where attenuating circumstances help to increase free will and make new choices. John Turtletaub's fine Disney film "The Kid", with Bruce Willis, might help you understand the process and its future consequences.

Having found a solution to your problem in the present you then have to put in place a new program, a creative input into your family group whose software you will be the first to install and which will become part of the baggage inherited by your children.

Let's return to Julia. Her older son, François, was an intelligent, successful boy. He became an air force officer and all went well. At 23 he met the woman who would become his wife and decided to leave the air force for other occupations. He passed a first exam, then failed one and failed another; he went for interviews; he was energetic but was never taken on. Married at 24, his first son was born. Jobless he looked after the baby while his wife worked to support the family. François keeps saying "It's as though I don't exist". (Your unconscious mind gives you accurate information, he had only to listen to the words to deduce it was merely a program and that he could create a different one.) (Often you can do this for yourself. Listen to your own words, it is only a program.)

So Julia, wanting to help her son, came to see me. She told me her story:

When I learnt that I was pregnant, in 1972, my husband didn't want any children. He so much didn't want them that he asked me to go to Geneva and see a psychiatrist in order to get a certificate which would allow me to have an abortion. Thirty years ago, this was a ploy for women who wanted an abortion, as they were still illegal then. I went to Geneva. I went into the empty waiting room but after a moment's thought, I came out again. I walked around the garden for a while and then I went into town, where I spent the day shopping. Back home that evening, I led my husband to believe that the psychiatrist had absolutely refused, because I was too young and because I was born to have children. He believed me. For the next nine months, he'd say to me: 'It's your problem if you're pregnant, you wanted it.' It was very painful for me, because almost every evening my husband went out with his friends, dancing or playing cards. He never took care of me and when I gave birth in Paris, he stayed in the south of France, where he'd been posted for work. At the time Francois was conceived, his father was also twenty-three.

Julia realised that Francois had unconsciously abided by his father's wish: not to exist. Should Francois be told this story so that he could release himself from it? Julia decided that he should, minimising and affirming so that, as she understood it, "there is no guilty party and no victim, each person acts according to the only unconscious access code that he possesses." His father was only 23 when he was conceived; he simply wasn't mature enough.

The most important thing is not what we were, nor what we are now, but what we will become. We are evolving beings. Don't see your parents for what they have been (they've already evolved a great deal), nor yet for what they are today, but for what they will be tomorrow!

Later on, picking up on Francois's words "it's as though I don't exist", I simply taught him to exist with the help of the tools that you will learn about below.

It is often difficult to admit that there are no guilty parties and no victims. How can we not be victims, when we arrive in this world according to our parents' or our grandparents' programs, and when we haven't asked for anything?…In theory, yes! That's why so many of us might think we are unlucky. Once again, this is the world of appearances.

In this diagram, the straight lines represent the course of normal life and the triangles, between conception and death, represent changes in one's state (for example, being in a state of illness and rediscovering a state of good health).

The universe already existed before we arrived (the small dashes); the earth had already been on quite a journey of its own. At the point where the father's sperm first meets the mother's egg (a point has no volume, length, width, or density, a point can exist without existing), you reach the world through a virtual double door. Two minutes before, the sperm hadn't met the egg; two minutes later, it has met it. Everything happens in an instant. Mathematicians say we should no longer talk about time, but about instants of time. Everything happens like lightning along the line of time.

From blastomere to embryo to foetus to baby to little child, you grow, your state changes. You are ill, you recover, you grow old, these are all changes of state that are of course visible with the naked eye, and you die in an instant. When your car wears out, there is no point trying to re-spray it, you just have to change it. Two minutes earlier you weren't dead, two minutes later, you are dead. You leave through a virtual double door. The universe continues to exist, the world continues on its journey. Death, that pejorative word, doesn't exist—it's another change of state which you can't see with the naked eye; and it's not because you can't see it that it doesn't exist. It's a crossing-over to something else. "Nothing is lost, nothing is created, everything is transformed", you haven't lost anyone, the thread hasn't been cut.

You exist in the universe before your conception and your arrival in the world. You stop existing in this world to return to the universe which has always existed, and you will always exist. Death is another change of state.

Bernard Wœsteland says that two fundamental questions preoccupied him: what is the meaning of life and should one be afraid of death? In an attempt to answer these questions, he read Dr. Moody's book "Life After Life". The doctor, who had managed to collect more than a hundred testimonials (which are therefore statistically valid), asserted that "Life exists after life. Death is no more than a short tunnel whose end soon comes into view."

Later, Bernard Wœsteland met a Swiss healer of about seventy who shared this story with him. I quote:

His mother was ninety-three, his forty-year-old unmarried daughter devoted herself to providing relief to the sick, following her father's footsteps. The three generations lived together in a small apartment full of antiquated things and nostalgic charm. About six months before his mother died, they were all discussing death quite openly and it was decided that the first one to go would send a sign to the others as soon as he or she got to the other world, if one existed. The mother was the first to go. They waited for the sign… Nothing… One month later, the son decided that, following tradition, he would take over the deceased's bedroom. He turned on the ceiling light and sparks flew out of it. He remained open-mouthed at the sight of the bulb—he had never seen anything like it…and nor, probably, will you. I had it in my hands: the inside was evenly lined in a smoky grey colour and, on the fullest part could be seen two interwoven letters, two Ms. His mother's name was Marthe-Marie.

Bernard adds that some people won't see any proof in this, but we are not on earth by chance or for no reason.

Most religions put it forward life after death as a hypothesis. After my friend Thierry died in a motorcycle accident, nine years ago, I went through a very bad patch. Searching for answers I investigated the world of energies, having studied theories of reincarnation in oriental philosophies. All that, to discover that we are the ones who choose our parents, before we are conceived, in order to undertake the evolutionary journey desired before our birth; and we are the ones who have planned our own obstacles. We have to realise that there are no problems, however great, that don't have a solution. (It's up to us to find it.)

The philosopher Henri Bergson considered the phenomenon of transmigration to be the most likely theory, and Bernard Wœsteland says:

> The soul could be seen as a state of consciousness, the personalisation of a living being, an invisible force inhabiting a very visible house, the body; it would leave the body at the moment of disintegration to wander for a while in the invisible world, where it would enter into a knowledge of the laws of life and, strengthened by this luggage, would come back to a new body in order to purify itself there and apply the new teaching it has received. It could, **depending on its will and its work, live a number of lives, and thus living side by side on this earth would be bodies harbouring old souls and young souls.** This explains the diversity of living beings, opposite and complementary, all necessary to the dynamics of life.

Imagine that you were acting in a play. Some actors play good guys, others bad guys. The play ends and you are all roundly applauded. You were a real hit. Would it occur to you to be angry with an actor who was playing a loathsome role? No, obviously not. And yet that's what you do. It's you who asked your parents to take on the role they played for you. You're no longer aware of it. That's why no one is a victim and no one is guilty. Make the most of your life, create something new, do better than your ancestors, move your clan forward, don't waste time examining all the mistakes and weaknesses of your elders, and stop criticising your parents. Hold on to what you have learnt, for you have come into the world to restore your clan and move it forward.

Your children are not your children. They are the sons and daughters of the call of life to itself. They come through you, but not from you. And, although they are with you, they do not belong to you. You can give them your love, but not your thoughts, for they have their own thoughts. You can foster their bodies but not their souls. You can strive to be like them, but don't try to make them like you. **Because life does not go backwards, nor does it linger at yesterday.** You are the bows from which your children, like living arrows, are propelled.

Khalil Gibran.

Because we can influence directly from brain to brain, we can do so with our children in a good way as long as we do it usefully and mindfully. Here is an example of positive influence:

In 1985 I was living in Tarbes with my children. My elder son, who was 13 at the time, enjoyed gliding. He was the youngest in the club. I was in the kitchen when the phone rang to tell me that a cyclone had sprung up, that my son was in the air and that he was in trouble. A mother's role at such a time is knot to give way to anxiety because, as has been said, you influence your child. I took myself off somewhere where I wouldn't be disturbed and fixed on a point on the door, to defocus my gaze and conjure up an internal, subjective depiction of a cyclone. I imagined my son's glider landing just beside it, unharmed. You repeat the same scenario, the wished-for outcome, fifty times. That's exactly what I did. The glider landed without mishap.

According to Professor Picard, who worked on the biosphere, the thoughts of a human being are, just like currents in an electronic calculator, oscillating at between 15 and 20,000 volts. When you think about someone you are sending 20,000 volts into the corner of their head. The current that comes back to you is twice as strong.

The danger posed by an anxious woman no longer needs to be proved. Imagine right now what you would like to happen to people you love. Imagine them as you would like them to be and turn this into an internal depiction (a scenario that produces an agreeable image). Take as long as you need, you'll get there.

The child is the extension of its parents. I remember a little boy of nine, Alexis, who couldn't add up or subtract, although he was good at multiplication. His teacher thought he was just being naughty, as did his parents. When he came to see me, I asked about the atmosphere at home. He told me that his parents, who came with him, quarrelled a lot. His mother explained that the quarrels were always about the same thing. During her pregnancy she hadn't worked. Her husband, a builder, would ask her every Saturday about the week's housekeeping money. He would add up the bills and shout at her for being spendthrift. So she would take away some of the bills. Both the adding and subtracting were sources of stress. On the 15th of the month, when the bank statement arrived, they could see that they were overdrawn, or nearly. The child's unconscious mind had found the solution. If his mother had known how to multiply the money, she would have done, so Alexis know how to multiply. Now if his parents didn't need to add up or subtract, they would get on, there would be love between them. That was what Alexis was doing—not adding, not subtracting—unconsciously, of course.

I simply explained all this to the child, getting him to see that it wasn't his problem and that he could let go of his solidarity. Then I gave him some addition and subtractions to do, with three and four numbers, which he was perfectly able to do. Understanding that it's a matter of recorded memory takes always all the blame.

You reproduce your parents' patterns of behaviour and you can change everything:

- By understanding (bringing to awareness)
- By behaving differently, so increasing your free will

In fact, our illnesses and our behaviour serve the purpose of setting right under our noses what we need to be aware of in order to cancel out family memories, overloaded with negative stress, that circulate within a clan. Illness helps repair and develop a clan. Sometimes our life programmes come to us from much further back, which might make you take an interest in **genealogy**. I can already hear people saying "Ah but I was born under X, or I'm a foreigner, I don't know anything." That's no problem.

Take a look at what's not right in your life, at what your faults are. Just be aware that you are reproducing patterns of behaviour, that you don't want to do so. That will be enough. You don't need historic detail.

Our ways of behaving and our illnesses provide effective information on the work we need to do to raise the level of our family or to understand our parents.

Long ago in Minnesota the Indian tribes (Native Americans) lived in tepees, as hunter-gatherers. When there was a serious drought, the Witchdoctor withdrew into a clearing, lit a fire, recited a prayer, and the next day it rained. The years went by, the Americans arrived and Indians were colonised. To begin with, put into reservations in wide open spaces, they were able to raise crops. On one occasion there was a serious drought and the Witchdoctor's son was sent for. They pleaded with him to do something to save the plantations. He said to himself "I have no clearing, but I will withdraw to a corner of the camp." He lit a fire, recited the prayer and the next day it rained. The years went by, the Indians were scattered in towns, some of them working in factories. They knew one another and often got together. On this occasion a very serious drought devastated the country. Knowing this story, the great-grandson of the Witchdoctor was sent for and people pleaded with him to intervene. He said to himself: "I have no clearing and don't know how to light a fire," but he withdrew to a quiet spot, recited the prayer, and the next day it rained.

More years went by, the Indians found themselves more and more scattered around America, in big towns and in the country; they knew one another less and less. This time an endless drought stretched over the country and was becoming more and more worrying. Someone heard the legend of the Indians and the great-great-great-grandson of the Witchdoctor was sent for. He lived in a skyscraper and they pleaded with him to intervene. He withdrew into the corner of a room and said to himself: "I have no clearing, I don't know how to light a fire and, besides, I don't know the prayer, but I know the legend." And the next day... it rained.

You see, you don't need the content of your stories, just the structure and the intention. It still works. You just need to update your present state (the parameters of your life) and decide to head off to a given desired state.

You may, however, be curious enough to want to discover your genealogy. There are many books available.

I want to make clear that it is not necessary to seek information from the past in order to explain the present. Instead you should establish an appropriate evolutionary future in the here and now and this will save the past. (This is our mission.)

Chris Morton and Ceri Louise Thomas, journalists and television reporters, have researched into crystal skulls (a Native American legend) and following a trip to Guatemala bring us their findings. In their scientific search, they report Einstein's theories, closing in on the idea that if we could travel faster than the speed of light, time would seem to travel backwards.

In other words we would be going back in time, something no human being has yet been able to do, though subatomic particles can.

In 1995, Professor Günter Nimtz conducted a subatomic experiment at the University of Cologne in Germany. His experiment consisted in splitting an information-bearing microwave signal in two. Half the signal was transmitted through the air and so, like all microwaves, travelled at precisely the speed of light. This signal arrived at its destination the very moment it was sent, like any other microwave. Nimtz tried something different with the other half of the signal. He placed what is known as a "quantum barrier" on its route. This is an electronic barrier whose function is to prevent the transmission of all subatomic particles, including microwave signals. His intention was to put an obstacle in the path of the signal, to prevent it getting through. In the event this was exactly the opposite of what happened.

In practice, the microwave signal sent through the quantum barrier travelled 4.7 times faster than light and arrived before it had even been sent. The results were staggering. Nimtz himself said that if we could build a quantum barrier across the universe, any message sent that way would travel faster than the speed of light and would in fact be travelling back in time. The message would reach the other side of the universe before it had even been sent.

The results of Nimitz's experiments are still the subject of debate among physicists. The important thing to keep hold of is the idea that roving subatomic particles can in effect dig a tunnel through a quantum barrier in such a way that they come out of this "time tunnel" before they have gone into it. The inference is that the precise position of an 'uncertain' quantum particle is determined **as much by its future position as by its past position, that there are 'imaginary waves of probability' with regard to the precise position of a given particle or rather 'of a quantum system' which travels forwards in time as much as backwards. And thus, in a sense, the present is determined as much by the future as by the past**.

The Mayas and many other Amerindian tribes portrayed time in the form of a circle, and an apparently very ancient Indian belief is that time is cyclical in nature rather than linear, going, as we in the west tend to see it, from the past to the future. For the Indians, communication across time is therefore possible.

It is preferable, here and now, to create information in a new mental map, to send it towards the past, rather than to dig up the past.

Barely five hundred years ago, the western world thought that the earth was flat. It took another five hundred years for western scientists to understand that time is not flat either. Time, too, is a great cycle.

The work we have to do in order to become the author of our own life will be to offer change to our elders, who didn't get the opportunity to change their own mental maps. Our duty is to do better than them. As I said above, we are constructed from our pasts and it has taken generations of men and women for you to be here today. Out of respect for all the members of this chain, improve your life and make it a masterpiece by thought and deed, so renewing the past and healing the wounds. That is why we need to spend a lot of time transforming the present, finding solutions, rather than going back into the past in an unnecessary search for errors or explanations.

To understand the evolution of the world and the fact that there are no victims and no culprits, we must become aware of the important role we have to play. Where do we come from? Who are we?

The four kingdoms

Since, according to Jean Charon, author of "World of Eons", we have a molecule of absolutely everything in us, we have been everything. This metaphor can enlighten us, since the energy bodies of all the living kingdoms are an integral part of man.

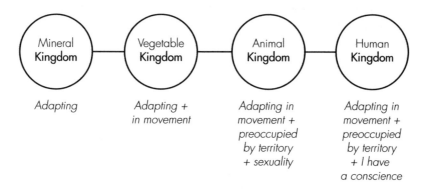

Mineral **Kingdom**	Vegetable **Kingdom**	Animal **Kingdom**	Human **Kingdom**
Adapting	*Adapting + in movement*	*Adapting in movement + preoccupied by territory + sexuality*	*Adapting in movement + preoccupied by territory + I have a conscience*

In the mineral kingdom

You learned to **adapt**. Wind, heat, cold, ice, storm—you adapted to the harshness of the weather (you had to, of course). Stones are worn in the direction of the water's flow. You remained some time in this kingdom. You're not going to get upset because a stone or a boulder has suffered. They adapted.

Then you passed into…

The vegetable kingdom

By now you have to know how to **adapt in movement**.

Trees bend in the direction in which the wind blows. Grasses at the river's edge go in the direction that the river flows.

Have you ever seen a tree resist? Grass that doesn't want to follow the direction of the current? But that's what you do when you don't go in the direction in which things are happening, when you refuse and resist. The tree might break, which is indeed what happens to some of you.

You remained for a certain length of time in the vegetable kingdom, then you passed into.

The animal kingdom

Now you must know how to adapt in movement, but this time with **territorial responsibility**, the sole preoccupation of the animal kingdom. Positioning oneself, marking and defending one's territory (BLADDER, HEART, KIDNEYS). The other new thing in this kingdom is sexuality. A male can mate with all the females. In some races there are no rules, in others the rules include homosexuality. Among wolves, only the leader of the pack can perpetuate the species. All the other wolves practise homosexuality, waiting for the, probably hypothetical, day when they become the dominant male.

In this animal kingdom you kill to eat, you gulp (wolf) food down so that others won't steal your prey. No one is upset if a lioness eats a gazelle, that a hyena kills any animal that hasn't run fast enough to escape, or that a monkey couples with his daughter.

Let's look at what cuckoos do. They lay their eggs next to the nest of a wagtail or a magpie; then because when one or the other is away looking for food, the cuckoo goes into that nest, gobbles an egg in an instant and replaces it with one their own. When the wagtail or the magpie returns, one of two things can happen: either the bird notices, or else it doesn't.

In the second case the female incubates the eggs and the cuckoo's is the first to hatch. When it is two days old it ejects all the other young occupants from the nest. The mother then feeds it until it's an adult, when it will fledge and fly away to its destiny without saying thank you—or maybe it does, I don't know.

If the magpie or wagtail does notice that it's not its own egg, it throws the unwelcome visitor out of the nest. But the cuckoo is watching. If this happens, it comes back and completely destroys the nest. Since all brains are linked to one another, cuckoos can't allow magpies or wagtails to survive which might have a memory that cuckoos usurp their place, or there would be no more cuckoos.

What cruelty! Imagine that in the human kingdom...

You stayed awhile in the animal kingdom, then you arrived in the...

The human kingdom

You should now be able to adapt, in movement, with knowledge of positioning, markings, territorial defence. You have some idea of sexuality, thanks to your memories, but this time you have a CONSCIENCE.

When you arrive in the human kingdom for the first time, yes you do have a conscience, but it's new and sadly underdeveloped. You're like a thirteen-year-old with muscles bursting to expand. The first step is to become aware of your conscience, which to start with is a totally blank canvas.

To satisfy all values: Love, Creativity, Compassion, Faithfulness, Spirituality, Self-awareness, Peace, Justice, Courage, etc... will take a long time. There are more than seventy values and you can't acquire them all at once.

Your arrival in the human kingdom is like your first day at kindergarten: you have everything to learn. True, you have two arms and two legs, but you go on killing, stealing, mating indiscriminately. The difference from the animal kingdom is that this behaviour is going to offend everyone.

Now would be a good time to realise that people do not have a different biological access code (from the animal kingdom), or a conscience to do things differently. There is danger, there are predators on the street; security doesn't come from other people but is up to us to develop (as we will discover below).

There is no place for surprise at certain forms of behaviour. Everything has a point, a useful purpose, all can be explained. One solution would be to be cautious oneself, and help other people, steering them towards evolving, rather than wasting one's time criticising or condemning them.

From kindergarten to high school, it'll take quite a while for you to bring together all the values of evolution, including compassion and love.

When you meet someone in the street (a map is not the same as being on the ground), you don't know what class that person is in. Whether you're in the sixth form or year one, there's no point showing off. You went through kindergarten too, but you don't recall anything about it. Have some compassion for those in the junior classes; I'm sure you wouldn't want to go back there.

If, nevertheless, curiosity is driving you to look into your genealogy, do it quickly. Crying or complaining because your grandmother was an alcoholic or your great-grandfather a murderer would be as ridiculous as crying because a cuckoo has destroyed a nest. It is, quite simply, evolution.

You just need to clarify "what needs evolving" or "what needs progressing" in terms of value. Self-awareness, mutual understanding, the success of the couple, professional success, money, success, kindness, which areas do you need to repair? Start to consider what you want to change in terms of your present life and experience.

Specialists didn't deprecate wooden trains or belittle the steam locomotive to get to the point where they were able to build the TGV (high speed train) and to go from Paris to Marseille in three hours. They quite simply imagined better and better, time and time again.

The flow of memories in a family clan

Everything works from brain to brain, from command centre to command centre, not only in a family clan, but throughout the universe.

As I explained earlier, you can choose to look for information from the past to explain the present or you can create the present/future, create a new mental map and send the information to the past, which will serve to repair your family clan. In that case, we no longer talk about Cause and Effect but about Effect and Cause.

Let's start with cause and effect. How can we explain that someone who gets divorced for the first time often meets the same type of partner, remarries, gets divorced again and never manages to live a fulfilling life as part of a couple ? Or how a brave and enterprising man can start a company, go bankrupt, optimistically start a new company, and fail again in the same way. Once again, we can say that we reproduce the same patterns, which often originated with our ancestors. The most important thing is not to realise that we are reproducing the same behaviour or the same misfortunes as our ancestors, but to realise that we are still using the same way of thinking in a similar situation, that we are reproducing the same mental strategies, the same maps. That is why we get the same results.

To change everything, think differently, acquire new strategies and succeed where our ancestors weren't able to. This is the target of your fate. Before acting (sending information to the past), let's look at the past in order to understand and explain the present.

Just as illness is only a possibility, so we are not inescapably condemned to reproduce a biological or psychological conflict. I was able to experience this with regard to weight loss, for example. In 1996, I weighed 140 lbs (I am 612 inches tall). My sister was much worse. My mother took us to the top specialists of the time. They were unanimous, "It's hereditary and what's more, your daughter has big bones." I decided I would do nothing in the same way as my grandmother. I don't eat like her, I don't think like her, I don't do anything like her. I lost 41 lbs and have weighed 99 lbs for the last thirty years. My sister, who did likewise, became a very

41

beautiful woman. And I realised, after I had slimmed down, that in fact I had small bones.

"Fate is the excuse of those who have no willpower." Hector Roland.

If I throw a ball at a wall, the wall returns it. Action/Reaction. If you keep the ball in your hand, that can't happen. Illness, problems result from actions. They are the natural consequence of an act which entails modifications in personality. Man, at the beginning of his acts, is a being in the process of becoming. "From out of perpetual creation, one creates oneself through one's acts."

We come in to the world with memories, with internal maps. How can an earlier energy intervene? Energy is said to be dynamic, energy in action, because it is confused with actions that are manifestations of it. We note the existence of earlier energy through the act itself and independently of it. It's an energy that doesn't act but that can act. It is static or potential energy. For example, imagine the reservoir of a hydro-electric plant. The dams in the mountains hold back a huge volume of water, weighing thousands of tons. When the valves on the intake pipes to the turbines are shut, the weight of this mass of water is inactive. It's in a static state. The work that it's going to do is still only potential, a possibility. If we open the valves, the water, under the action of the weight, gushes into the pipes and turns the turbines. The whole plant will be set in motion. Accordingly, the static energy of the water in the reservoir will pass into the dynamic state.

The same is true, in whatever form energy presents itself (heat, electricity), the action, the discernible manifestation of dynamic energy, presents itself at one time in an active mode and at another in a passive mode, depending on whether this action is carried out or undergone.

I beat or I am beaten, I love or I'm loved, I think for myself or I am subjected to collective thinking, I speak or I listen. When a body is subjected to an action, it reacts. It goes from passive to active.

In the universe, actions and reactions are inextricably linked. You get back what you throw, and it is this linking that constitutes the law of causality that governs our world. You reap what you sow.

Once we have understood our responsibility in this process, we create our life. It is up to us not to reproduce the mistakes of the past, and that's why our life path serves to repair and save our clan.

"Success is the process by which we strive to become 'more'." The path to success is always under construction. It's a process, not an ultimate goal to be achieved.

Genealogy and remembered cycles of course help us to understand the logic. It is easier to forgive when we become aware that evolution is slow and gradual. Algebra can't be explained to a four-year-old child. He'll begin, step by step, with the basics: letters, numbers, arithmetic, dictation, etc. There is therefore no culprit, no victim. People around us and we ourselves do not have a different biological access code to do anything other than what we do...In the universe, everything is right and everything can be explained.

If your brilliant brain doesn't have, in its archives, a programme for success, for abundance, for life as a fulfilled couple, for professional success, it's not going to invent it. It can only operate on the givens from you or that it already possesses. So in the first instance, to observe one's life and to become aware of the contents of one's baggage is interesting. Just decide that you won't put up with it any longer, that you will do better than your parents. Create a pleasant feeling around this idea; this will be enough to wipe out memories.

In the second instance, you should pass from the present state to the desired state. To do that, you will have to dream and to state clearly how you want to live differently from the way you live now. This will be the beginning of a new start.

Many people are able to say what they don't want or what annoys them but few can specify what they would like instead. Your unconscious brain awaits your orders and needs to understand the precise statement of your wishes.

This is what we are going to specify together. Let's go towards the creation of a new future, and at last live a high-quality existence.

CHAPTER 11

CREATING THE LIFE YOU WANT

The faculties of the brain

Why is it that people who become depressed still find themselves in the same state, or even worse, 20 years later, despite regular visits to a psychiatrist?

It is quite simply because no-one has managed to take them from their present state (unhappy in love, no money, I don't like my body, I'm ugly, I'm persecuted, I don't like my job, I can't communicate, etc) to a desired state (i.e. what they would like instead). All that time, they talked about their problem, obviously reinforcing the same answer, whilst clinging to the same beliefs. Twenty years down the road they still haven't met their soul mate, still have no money, still haven't attempted to change their appearance, still feel persecuted and ugly and have never tried to learn to communicate efficiently and elegantly with others.

In my view, the art of therapy is to help people change their lives and go beyond their limits. To teach them to meet the right people, how to form a lasting couple, how to improve their appearance and condition. In short, having them spend 90% of their time on the solutions rather than on the problems.

Let's imagine we're going jogging together in the countryside. You are running in front of me when suddenly you fall into a deep, narrow hole with slippery sides. What do you prefer? Would you rather I study **why** you fell into this hole or **what I am going to do get you out?**

I can spend a long time studying the why aspect and you may well die down there if I don't find a way to get you out.

If you are reading this book it means that it is the right moment for you to let go of the "why", the "I feel bad", and concentrate on the "what am I going to do to feel better?"

I noticed that when I used to tell people that happiness really exists, that like a magnet they could attract what they wanted, I very often got the reply: "Don't exaggerate".

But it is true! You may think: "you have to believe in it to start with". Wrong. You need to study it not believe in it.

Do you need to believe that the light will come on when you press the switch? Obviously not because you know it will. However, if you had been frozen in 1700, put into hibernation and unfrozen today would you need to believe everything you see or learn? You would be right to be dumbfounded.

I would like to teach you how to use your brain/computer, your untapped potential to drastically change your life now.

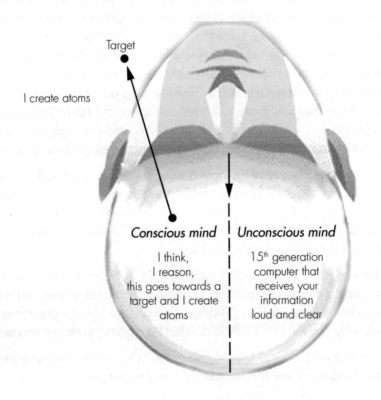

Target

I create atoms

Conscious mind | **Unconscious mind**

I think,
I reason,
this goes towards a
target and I create
atoms

15th generation
computer that
receives your
information
loud and clear

As you saw in the previous paragraph, you consciously think, reason and are under the impression you are logical. Your conscious mind is linked to the solar plexus, to the world of emotions. Our reality is our very own reality and is the result of our distorting observation. Where do our emotions come from? From the way in which we perceive others or events, from our interpretations.

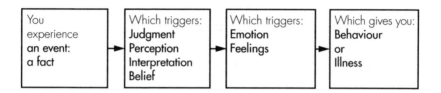

| You experience an event: a fact | → | Which triggers: Judgment Perception Interpretation Belief | → | Which triggers: Emotion Feelings | → | Which gives you: Behaviour or Illness |

Therefore, other people are not responsible for our emotions or our behaviour. They are quite simply triggered by the way in which we interpret events.

According to quantum physics, what happens in our world depends on the way we observe it. And what is important is that an observed phenomenon can not be dissociated from the device that is used to measure it. This means that what you observe cannot be dissociated from yourself. **Reality is therefore created by the observer.**

Einstein said: "the real problem is that we don't know what reality is. We only know it through its physical description". Everything we see with our eyes is interpreted with our filters and we deform reality. As the French writer St. Exupéry said: "what is extremely important is everything we can not see with the naked eye, everything that is invisible".

Conscious mind: when you think about something, even something very simple, you perform an action and this action has a result. There are billions of people on earth who think and we can not "not think" (except for moments when we use letting-go techniques).

Each time you think, you emit elementary particles in the form of wave bursts that spiral towards a target at a certain speed.

Jean Guitton has shown that:

An elementary particle exists in the form of a 'wave burst'. In other words, everything happens as if there were an infinite number of particles, each of them having a trajectory, a speed, a position etc. However, when observed, the wave function collapses and only one of these vast numbers of particles materialises, thereby cancelling out all the parallel particles. And at the moment an event takes place in the long chain of phenomena that have formed the history of our universe, an infinite number of virtual events fade away, swallowing up a myriad of ghost worlds in its wake. Only our unique and indivisible reality remains. This provokes the collapse of the wave function characterising a phenomenon. It is quite simply the act of observing.

Radio France-Inter, Monte Carlo radio, the BBC, Rai Uno; there are no wires in the universe. These are frequencies, wavelengths. Let's go back to this important expression: "when you think, you emit elementary particles in the form of wave bursts that spiral towards a target at a certain speed". Depending on what you are thinking, on the intensity you put into it and even on how often you do it (often, every day or repeatedly), you are joining with millions of people who think like you. Thought is everywhere in an instant. You receive a frequency, a wavelength and you create atoms. Some atoms fly off with all the subjects you deal with during the day whereas others remain.

We emit and we receive. If you are tuned in to Radio 4 you can't listen to a concert on Classic FM. You will agree on that. Yet how many of you remain tuned in to criticism, rejection, fear, boredom but would really like to hear programs on wealth, health, success? It's not possible.

According to the theories of Jean Guitton, the reason why certain atoms fly off whereas others remain is only because they are being observed, because we think about them.

If you keep thinking strongly and repeatedly about a pleasant or a dreaded subject every day, you will create and experience it. If you stop thinking about it, it flies off.

This means that you should spend your time thinking about "**what you want**" rather than thinking about everything you don't like, don't want or that frightens you.

What is thought? According to Einstein, the speed of an object is limited to that of light and all objects in the universe move around in time and space. It is a generalised speed in the four dimensions, made up of a speed in time and a speed in space.

When stopped (at rest), time passes (hence, we move only through the time dimension and not at all in the spatial dimensions).

However, when we are in movement, the trajectory is divided between space and time. What is given to space has been subtracted from time.

For immobile observers (in space) the object seems to travel more slowly in time.

Thought is not an object and therefore has no mass. It is elusive and can travel faster than the speed of light. According to Einstein's restricted theory of relativity, the speed of light is a physical limit we cannot go beyond. Only photons, which are particles with no mass, transport their energy at this speed to create light. For a particle with a mass to reach the speed of light, it would have to be endowed with infinite energy, which is impossible. According to Einstein's calculations, time slows down for those who approach the speed of light.

For quantum physics, nothing is preventing us from envisaging particles that would travel faster than the speed of light in a vacuum. These purely theoretical particles called tachyons are believed to exist naturally above speed of light limiting our physical universe. In any case, and according to the theory, they are said to be made of a strange matter with properties that are very different from those of our universe.

In our reality, cause always precedes effect. Now, if we had a tachyonic ball and a child threw it through the window, we would see the glass break before the child threw the ball because the speed of the ball is greater than that of light. This is like saying that we can see the effect before the cause.

Thought is not palpable and differs from what can be observed in our known universe. Thought is believed to be tachyonic in essence, according to Regis Dutheil. It is believed to travel faster than light and is everywhere in an instant (in time past, present, future and in space).

It is important today to change our reality and work in this sense: Effect/Cause. As we have seen in the first paragraph, making an assessment of the life we are living means solving the effect so as to weed out the cause.

When you think about your everyday activities (according to the scientists in John Hopkins University, Maryland) you think at 224 miles per hour (the result of an experiment where 174 electrodes were placed on the head of a young man). So thought is said to travel at 224 mph.

Here are a few examples of banal thoughts: "I need to buy bread, I'm going to pick up my son from school, I forgot to telephone". These things find their own solutions because quite naturally and without you realising it, your unconscious mind organises them, makes your limbs move and so on. When you want to pick up an object or move around, you simply emit this desire, you let go and your brain does the rest. You don't think: "I need to hold out my hand, bend my fingers, lift up my foot", because you may well miss the target. The role of thought is to think and the role of the brain is to provide the means. It is when you want to find the solution all by yourself, in your thoughts, that you create stress. This stress is often very hard to manage and illnesses frequently appear because you have created a problem.

The problem is not in the problem. The "wanting to" find solutions in your thought creates the problem and it is at this instant that thought can attain tachyonic speed. In our body we have two major organs; the lungs and the brain. The role of the lungs is to breathe and that of the brain is to find solutions. The brain operates on an arithmetical and a geometrical basis. As for the lungs, whether you are breathing mountain air or exhaust fumes, they function. They don't say: "I don't want to breathe this air, it's not healthy". It's the same for the brain. It seeks perfect solutions to the image it received and the words pronounced. It doesn't reason on data, it carries out its function.

It is very important to respect two parameters:

- The nature of your thought which, at tachyonic speed is everywhere at once in the same way as light.
- The words used which conjure up an immediate internal image, with the unconscious mind looking for an outcome.

You are similar to millions of people who think like you on this planet. Either you materialise the exact subject of your thought in your biology (i.e. your body) or you get the result in your life.

In summary: putting all the theories together; when you think about something you emit elementary particles in the form of wave bursts that spiral towards a target at a certain speed. You are similar to millions of people who think like you, you are part of a frequency, a wavelength and you create atoms. Some atoms fly off and others stay.

The first step towards "Creating the Life You Want" will be to think consciously and to observe what you would really like. Write it down, say it aloud using the appropriate words and trust your unconscious mind to fulfil it. Similarly, when a problem arises in your life, all you need do is hand it over to your unconscious mind so it can deal with it.

Between the moment you see a real image, the instant you turn it into an internal mental representation and the moment this image is recorded by the brain, roughly a quarter of a second passes (250 to 300 thousandths of second). This was established in an experiment in John Hopkins University in Maryland in 1998.

When something happens to you, it is either what you really want or what you fear the most (it is intense observation that counts, plus the image (the internal subjective representation we have of it), plus the sound (the internal dialogue; what we say to ourselves) and the associated feelings).

A mother picks up the dictation her son did at school and says: "I don't understand, why do you make so many mistakes?" 16 mistakes.

Now, there's a good question. If the child knew why, he wouldn't make so many mistakes! Because his mistakes are being observed, he will make more and more. But if his mother says to him: "you do have four words right!" the child can then start observing the contrary and he will begin to write more and more words right without even trying.

Everything comes down to the observation, the image and the internal representation.

When someone says: "I hate roses", the speaker immediately conjures up an image of roses and it may very well be that this is the flower that people are always giving her. It would be better for her to say the name of her favourite flower.

Someone else says, "I love roses", the image is the same. The only difference is that this person will most likely get what she likes.

If you are afraid of being burgled, you are connected to burgling. If you are afraid of being ill you emit on the illness wavelength. We could just as easily find a different radio or television channel and tune in to health, success or safety and security. Doing the opposite often seems simpler.

We are capable of consciously provoking disasters. We want to be in control of our lives but we don't really know how. We influence our unconscious mind a great deal with all our presuppositions, interpretations, fears, doubts and guessing what the future holds.

Now, what about our **unconscious mind**? It doesn't think or reason and has a logic all of its own. It is unaware of our reality, of fiction, of the virtual and the imaginary. Our unconscious mind works in symbols and metaphors. Metaphors help create links and give meaning. With his fables, the writer La Fontaine managed to say everything he wanted to the king.

Many school books go against the way in which the unconscious mind functions. This explains why many children take no interest in them as they can't see any link with their everyday lives.

Milton Erickson (the father of Erickson hypnosis) said that there is a conscious part of us that carries thoughts, emotions (inner states and feelings), beliefs and programs. At the same time we also have other parts made up of programs, conclusions and different memories. We are all of that. This conscious part is at the helm but is not necessarily wise and its job is not to find solutions.

The unconscious is believed to be divided into two: first of all the past and our experiences and also the observer of our conscious which is believed to have access to everything. It doesn't intervene unless called upon. It is like an informed unconscious: a wise, knowledgeable and vigilant guide. It observes what we do, why we do it and is believed capable of intervening, opening the barrier to allow solutions through to a level of change.

But the conscious, organised and rational mind that has acquired beliefs blocks the path of the unconscious, preventing it from intervening at the appropriate moment. This explains why Milton Erikson wanted to get around this conscious part that thinks it knows everything. The idea was to take it off its guard and then look for the means to solve people's problems in their unconscious mind.

The solution to everything you are experiencing today lies in a beneficial change and this is what I propose to do together.

When you have thought about your subject, emitted particles in the form of wave bursts, made atoms and joined with the millions of people who think like you, the information remains in your unconscious mind. It receives it loud and clear. Just like a magnet, it will then attract all the solutions and circumstances to prove you are right. You will always be right, your mind does not judge. It patiently awaits your orders so it can carry them out, whatever they may be.

Obviously, your mind needs a little fuel; the oxygen from your blood and a bit of glucose. This means eating healthy food because the richer the food in vitamins and mineral salts, the greater chance you have of reasoning perfectly, of being very efficient.

We have enormous potential and unlimited resources without being consciously aware of this. And for some of you, if you are aware of it, at school you didn't learn how to use it.

Here is an important pre-supposition of Neuro-Linguistic Programming (NLP): all individuals possess the necessary resources and potential within them to bring about any changes they desire.

You have 28 billion computers ready to go. This is indeed what they do; they "go" but not necessarily in the right direction. In everyday life you can cause disasters simply by pressing unwittingly on any key.

Now, imagine you wanted to print a pay slip on a computer that doesn't have the appropriate software. You can't. Or make a Powerpoint presentation without this software. It's quite simply not possible. You have the desire and the will but not the program.

What this shows is that if you don't have the right program to create a happy couple or a successful business, your brain isn't going to invent it. But, it is there to solve enigmas or problems as well as to create a new program and reach a new target.

Your unconscious mind is an automatic mechanism and can function just as well in failure mode as in success mode. Everything depends on the data you give it to process and the goals you fix for yourself. It is a solution-seeking mechanism. Beware of your internal images because, as I have said before, this automatic mechanism asks no questions, nor does it think about the data it receives. It simply operates, period.

The role of conscious thought is to know what is true and to check that what you are thinking is indeed what you want.

So decide what you want, now.

When you pronounce a word, the internal image must match your desire. Keep an eye on the target and let your unconscious mind operate. You do this quite naturally, and much too often, for many negative things. You should simply consciously emit precise desires and above all (and we will come back to this several times) do not concern yourself with the way in which they'll be fulfilled.

"I know or I don't know" is the motto of your mind. Do not make ambitious plans, either negative or positive. It is just as absurd to claim you will succeed as it is to be afraid of failing. You have no idea. These are predictions, auto-suggestions with no logical reality.

When you have a desire or objective there are two ways NOT TO REACH IT.

We have an imaginary time-line in our mind:

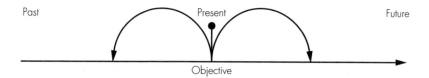

Past   Present   Future

Objective

- The first way to miss the target: go back 35 minutes into the past, rremind yourself of all your failures and bring them back to the present as markers. This is a very good way to fail. The mistakes of the past belong to the past. At that time you weren't capable of determining an objective or organising your thinking. Things are different today. You are learning about the faculties of the brain, you can accept that you have all the required resources within you to succeed and that if you don't have them your mind can acquire them.

- The second way: project yourself 45 minutes into the future whilst asking yourself this stupid question: "Will I manage?" Your mind has no idea because it is not in the future.

- The only possible moment is **here and now.**

State your desire and ask yourself this initial question:

"WHY DO I WANT THAT, what is my intention in wanting that?"

Answer this question before going on to the next one:

"What is the GOAL of wanting what you want?"

After this, here is the only possible question here and now: "What can I do now to reach my goal?"

Your mind will help you move up in small, easy stages because it is specialised in processes and is perfectly capable of finding solutions in the present. At each stage ask yourself the same question: "what can I do now?" You will get to the top of your ladder and will have reached your goal without having had the time to ask yourself: "Will I manage?"

It is like a dance with the unconscious mind. You then act on the basis of the ideas that come to mind. They will come in the right order. Follow your unconscious mind, it has a lot to offer.

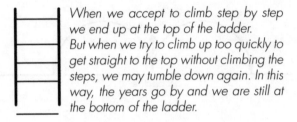

When we accept to climb step by step we end up at the top of the ladder.
But when we try to climb up too quickly to get straight to the top without climbing the steps, we may tumble down again. In this way, the years go by and we are still at the bottom of the ladder.

You came into the world to climb a mountain. This is the path of your destiny. All the obstacles you meet are learning processes. You have the whole of your lifetime to reach the summit.

The book "The Path of Your Life" by Dan Millman, published by Roseau will help you understand the path of your destiny. Using numerology, he explains how to travel your path and how to get to the end.

The goal of your destiny

All the obstacles you meet are learning processes.

Ideas are not changed by will-power but by other ideas

Which frequency are you tuned in to?

Which frequency are you broadcasting on?

Decide now which radio station you want to tune in to. Broadcast on the right frequency. What you receive in return will obviously depend on the level of your broadcast. Have you ever played with an echo in the mountains? If you shout through your cupped hands "I love you", the echo that comes back is "love love love love". Have you ever heard a word come back that is not one of those you shouted? Of course not.

It is the same in your life.

Our five senses

You have five senses through which your unconscious mind receives information. These will be used to create the life you want: sight, hearing, touch, smell and taste. You experience these five senses both internally and externally.

1 – You are visual

You are **externally visual** (you see what is around you).

You are reading this book right now.

You are **internally visual** (you have an internal camera).

You can imagine a beach, your car or your bedroom and picture it in your mind. If I say to you "don't see a giraffe", you have already seen it even though I asked you not to. Your mind is obliged to see a giraffe before it can stop seeing it. It doesn't know "how not to". The internal representation is automatic. To create a mental image of this sentence: "don't think about your mother-in-law", you have to think about her in order to stop thinking about her. This is why, when we say to a child: "don't go and play on the edge of the swimming pool", the child goes because the immediate image that comes to his unconscious mind is the "edge of the pool". The mother will think her child is defying her but if she asks him to go and play in the sandpit he will most certainly do so.

I was sitting in a train, at the platform. The passengers were all getting on. A woman arrived in the corridor with her daughter aged about five. As there were suitcases sticking out she said to the little girl "careful you don't fall over". The little girl caught her foot in the straps and went headlong onto the floor. Her mother could have said: "look where you're going and pick your feet up".

Depending on the mental image you create, your mind is capable of attracting everything necessary for the image to become real.

Negatives are only conceivable consciously and via our internal discourse. None of our other senses—hearing, feeling, touch and taste—can imagine a reality that is negative. "Do not hear the music", you will hear it immediately. "Don't feel the pressure of your shirt on your skin", you will obviously feel it and so on.

Your unconscious mind doesn't make any difference between what you see on the outside and the images created on the inside. Everything is true as far as it is concerned.

Like a magnet, it will attract everything needed to make things happen. Events will go in the same direction as your images.

Your mind makes no judgement.

To create the life we want, we will first of all create images—internal, subjective representations of the beauty and harmony we aspire to. Conjure up images that are clear, precise, in colour and close to you. You may see nothing at first but this is quite natural. You are not used to doing this type of exercise. Imagine your bedroom, your car and other familiar objects and little by little images will come to you. To do this, stare at a fixed point in the room or close your eyes.

2 – You are auditory

You are **externally auditory** (you can hear and listen to external sounds and noise around you).

You are **internally auditory** (you can speak to yourself, you have an internal dialogue).

In the same way as for vision, your mind won't make any difference between what you hear externally and what you say to yourself. Yet again, like a magnet, it will attract all the circumstances to you so that things will happen.

What is the meaning of the expression: the **word** "is" the **thing**?

It means that **you experience what you say.**

e.g. "I'm afraid of falling, I'm afraid of falling, I'm afraid of falling". The more afraid you are of falling, the more your stress increases and the more the image created is that of you on the floor. The only thing the mind can do is make you fall. You are on the floor and are no longer afraid. **The fear of the thing creates the thing.** The fear of failure creates failure and the fear of illness creates illness. It's a pity you didn't think of being afraid of success. This would have resulted in you succeeding.

The internal image, the words you use in your head and the created emotion that goes with it are a good recipe for creating events and getting outcomes. We will see this later on.

A three year old boy enjoys riding his bike with two small wheels at the back. He can go fast and well. One day his father says: "OK son, let's take these little back wheels off, you're 4 now and old enough to manage without them". The little boy is afraid of falling of course and that is exactly what happens as he can't find his balance. He will soon adapt and find his own natural solutions to make it easier to learn and curiously the internal image changes. He creates an image of what he wants, i.e. to stay upright on his bike.

The perfect solution to the desire for what we really want is to have it. The perfect solution to the fear of what we do not want is also to have it so that the stress will disappear. The mind is there to find solutions, including those needed to survive.

Your computer does not pay attention to spelling, e.g. "percussion" is the same as "per cushion". Poets are very kinesthetic people (feelings).

If I say to you "I **want**", you can't see anything, you have no images. "I **don't want**" and still you see nothing.

Now, "I don't want a coffee," and along comes an image of a cup and of coffee. Whether you like it or not, the mind will always picture the image of the word and make links between what is said and your life or between what you see and what it knows. The image attached to it is the same whether you say "I want" or "I don't want".

A young woman says: "I really don't want to meet someone macho". Immediately her mind will look for a way to have her meet someone macho and her experience will be exactly the opposite of what she wanted. This woman will think she is unlucky because she doesn't know that the word "IS" the thing and that you experience what you say.

"I don't want to be ill", is the magic formula for the mind to seek out ways to be even more ill. This sentence could be expressed as "I really want to be in good health". The unconscious mind will not reverse the sentence by itself. It is up to you to say exactly what you want.

Every day we use words to describe how we feel, to express our desires and our interpretation of events. We use words that influence not only us but also those around us, whether we are aware of it or not. According to the research of Jack Can Field (1982), a child receives roughly 460 negative comments or reprimands per day compared to only 75 positive and motivating ones.

INDIRECT COMMUNICATION: a conscious or unconscious way to pass on messages

If we use spoken language to communicate, why not make it even more effective and constructive by using **words that enhance, stimulate and lead to success?** It would be great to rid our vocabulary of toxic or parasitical words, i.e. those that are slowly but surely destructive.

In our childhood fairy tales, the nasty queen cast a spell on the hero (using what is called analogical marking). This is a gesture coupled with a magic formula sometimes going as far as a curse. For some of you, your family circle has cast this type of spell on you quite often. No-one is aware of this but the magic formula-turned-scathing-remark has made inroads into your mind. The prophecy comes true.

"You are really useless—you'll never get anywhere—you're hopeless—stop making a fuss—you're no good at… etc.

Then you take over:

"What an idiot I am—I'll never manage—I'm unlucky—I'm going to be taken for a ride again…"

When learning some of the indirect communication techniques created by Milton Erickson (indirect communication means getting the message across without the conscious mind either noticing or opposing it), you will notice that we have often done it naturally and that it has sometimes been a disaster (of course, these techniques should only be used in an ethical, therapeutic context to help people).

For example, if you talk in a relatively monotonous way, leave a short silence then suddenly say a phrase or a word very loudly and clearly and then carry on as before, which words will leave their mark on the unconscious mind of the person you are speaking to? Only those you have pronounced followed by a "blank" (space) and with a different tone of voice, louder and more assertive than the rest.

To summarise: **monotonous tone – blank – important word – blank – monotonous tone.** This is called **"sprinkling"**.

Let's take an example: a father is explaining maths to his son in a monotonous voice. "I don't understand, I've explained this to you 10 times" (blank) then loudly **"Are you stupid or something?"** (blank)—monotonous "bla bla bla…"

Well done! The damage is done…the boy thinks he's "stupid".

It is also important to teach children to use "strong" rather than "weak" words because emotions are tied to words.

Try asking a schoolboy: "Do you think you're intelligent?"

He hesitates before answering. He's not really sure and the answer won't be clear: "yes, a little" or "I don't know" or clearly "no". But he needs to be **sure** about this in order to succeed. He doesn't know that his unconscious mind is following everything he thinks and says.

We can ask him to explain the word "intelligent". Everything depends on the explanation we give to words. Everyone has their own definition.

"What does being intelligent mean for you"? Or "what would it take for you to be intelligent?"

In general, the answer is prohibitive, e.g. "I would need to understand everything immediately or to assimilate all subjects, to be able to answer any question, to master this or that quickly…"

With definitions like that I'm also far from being able to consider myself intelligent!

Teach your children to adopt definitions that are simple for the mind. Being intelligent, for example, could be defined as "being open to many things, developing and stimulating our imagination". The unconscious mind will assimilate this and the child will become increasingly intelligent.

Here is another possible question: "Are you brilliant?" A categoric "no!" "What would have to happen for you to be brilliant?" Now the explanation is even more prohibitive. There is not much chance this person will become brilliant one day.

My brother always used to say, even when he was very young, "I'm brilliant, I'm brilliant". Today he is a well known writer. One day I asked him: "What does being brilliant mean for you,?" He answered: "To be able to laugh at my own stupidity and at other people's". Obviously, being tuned to this wavelength and with such a simple definition, his brain had led him in that direction. He really is brilliant.

A **"criterion"** is a word, a small value (nice, intelligent, good pupil, practical...). A word is abstract. However, the explanation you give to a word is concrete and is called the "complex equivalence". Many conflicts between people are conflicts of value equivalents.

You very often share the same values and the same criteria as those close to you but what you don't know is that the definition of a word is totally different from one person to another, even between two people who are very intimate. You have always thought that the people you speak with can understand what you say, but this is not necessarily the case.

Since birth you have seen things that others haven't seen. You have heard people say different things and you have had emotions that nobody else has felt. You have received an education from your parents and teachers. You have filtered all this information and adopted your own system of beliefs. In short, you have created your own "model of the world".

Each model of the world is unique. We are all unique because we have all seen, heard and felt different things and we have all drawn a conclusion from our experiences. This is why the words we pronounce are only a surface, a code used to express ourselves. This surface is linked to real-life experiences which form its deep structure (the explanation).

When you hear words and expressions used by someone speaking to you, you interpret them using your own filters and beliefs. You import them into your own experience which has no connexion with the other person's real life experiences. The definition you give to it is your very own and may be totally different from another person's. Worse still, after interpretation, you understand the intention of the message even less. Because of this, we may think that people have negative intentions when this is not at all the case (consider, for example, the reputation of mothers in law who are only doing their best to look out for their children but who are often seen as terrible old battle-axes).

If the explanation of one word differs from one person to another, giving rise to a good deal of argument and misunderstanding, imagine an entire speech! We see couples who thought they understood each other after 15 years of marriage. Not a bit of it. In fact, they never understood anything. Incredible!

Sylvain, a young man of 18 who began studying NLP at the same time as a friend of his told me one day: "my friend Frank knows me very well, we understand each other very well". "We'll see about that," I replied.

I then asked him to tell Frank about his plans for the future. Sylvain began: "when I leave my parents I'll get a big apartment". "OK", says Frank. Sylvain goes on: "A big, quiet apartment". "Fine", says Frank.

I put a stop to the discussion at that moment and asked Frank what he had understood, seeing as he knows his friend so well. "So, you want a big apartment, I think 150m². "Are you crazy!" said Sylvain. "The bedroom I have now is 15m², I'd be very happy with 60m²". And what about the word calm? "Considering your family lives next to a forest, with birds and stuff, I suppose you want the same thing". "Not at all," replied Sylvain. "Quiet for me means living on the top floor of an apartment block in the town centre with no-one above me".

If Frank had been an estate agent, he would have taken this young man to see apartments that were nothing like what he wanted, saying: "I took him to see what he wanted". Far from it!

One of your friends says: "I know a great restaurant". You take your family there and are not at all impressed. The food isn't to your taste and it's very noisy. A few days later you meet your friend and ask him "what specifically is a good restaurant for you?" or "what does it mean for you, a restaurant good?"

"For me, a good restaurant is one that gives you a lot to eat", he answered.

So you see, it's well worth asking what someone understands by a word rather than interpreting or buying into an idea that you will later dislike.

So, to avoid arguments, or rather in order to get on well, there are two questions to remember to ask before presupposing anything, especially anything negative.

"What does 'X' mean for you?" or "What specifically is it like for you, this or that?"

You can also say: "What I understand from what you have just said is…" "Is that what you wanted me to understand?"

You will most certainly be surprised by the answer.

Also, check on the words you use for yourself because you will always become what you have just said and what you believe you are. Change your vocabulary and give your words definitions that are easy to explain.

Be nice to yourself and use words that are enhancing encouraging, constructive and positive where you are concerned.

To create the life you want, you will need to use reasoning and say the words that you desire.

Another indirect communication technique used by Milton Erickson is that of "presuppositions": **when — as soon as — the day after the day when…**

A doctor who says to one of his patients: "when you start to walk again take it step by step",(presupposition: I am going to walk again). Or "when you want to close your eyes, close them when you feel the time is right", (presupposition: I am going to close my eyes).

Once you have defined your objectives, thanks to the next paragraph, present arguments. "When I have…" "As soon as I…" "The day after the day when I"… etc.

"The right word is a powerful agent. Whenever we come upon one of those intensely right words…the resulting effect is physical as well as spiritual, and electrically prompt".

Mark Twain

3 – You are kinesthetic

You are **externally kinesthetic**: (i.e. external sensations and feelings): warmth, cold, the wind, a caress, a slap etc. In fact, all external sensations.

You are **internally kinesthetic**: (these are emotions, feelings and inner states). You are happy, not happy, pleased, not pleased…

You can't feel something if you see nothing, if you hear nothing or if you feel nothing externally.

What we have seen above can be summarised as follows:

Event → Judgement → Emotion → Behaviour

Revision: people or events are not responsible for your emotions, your feelings or your behaviour. It is the way in which you interpret events. Your judgements, your beliefs and your perceptions trigger your emotions and feelings.

When something you consider "terrible" happens to you, "accepting it" is really not the right reaction. How can a mother accept that her daughter has been raped or that her son has died? "Understanding" is the only way to let go and then acceptance becomes natural.

The first thing to do is look for the useful function in the event because there is always one.

To show you that our emotions are the result of a perception or a judgement I'll tell you about one of Maxie Maulsby's experiments. He was studying beliefs and the effect they have in our life.

On the morning we arrived for a seminar, breakfast trays had been put out for each of us. It smelled really tasty and we were all very thankful. When we had all put a tray on our knees, Maxie said "Don't touch it. I spat and urinated in all the cups of tea and coffee". Of course we all felt sick and no-one touched a thing on the tray.

Maxie then asked: "does your emotion come all by itself or is it your perception that triggers your feelings?".

Even after telling us it was all a joke, none of us would touch anything on the trays.

When you go to consult a therapist it's because you think that something is wrong. You would like the therapist to do something for you. After several years of therapy you may say: "I feel better". But as long as the beliefs linked to the roots of your distress have not changed, you will still have the same emotions as on the very first day of therapy (negative and painful emotions no doubt). One of your major concerns in life will be to change your perceptions, interpretations and beliefs (see chapter: "Toolbox").

Moreover, as your mind can't create an image representing something negative, remember that when you say "I mustn't get angry" or "I'm not afraid", your mind will immediately provide you with the feeling of being annoyed or afraid. **Pronounce the words you want immediately, you will feel the emotions latch on to them.**

In the chapter on sychronicities, you will find the appropriate question to ask yourself when something (apparently) terrible happens to you. "What is extraordinary about this? What would be extraordinary about this if I really wanted there to be something extraordinary?" You will see that everything is wonderfully orchestrated in the universe. Everything is extraordinary, even if this isn't the initial impression you get.

Here is a **fact**: you are with a friend on holiday in delightful surroundings. You are swimming quite far out to sea because the water is heavenly and the weather so lovely. Your friend has stayed on the beach. Suddenly, he shouts out: "someone said there's a shark in the water!"

- A **belief** sets in. If you really believe there's a shark.
- Your **emotion** suddenly becomes "fear and panic".

- Your **behaviour**: you have never swum to the shore so fast in all your life.

But if your friend then says: "April fool" your fear disappears.

So, there is no point acting on an emotion. As long as you believe what you believe, your emotion won't change.

You can change your beliefs (see different definitions in the chapter: "Toolbox"). You can even overcome the childish suggestions of the unconscious and change its content by using an appropriate technique.

Re-evaluate your beliefs: if you carry remorse or guilt around with you, look at the causes and convince yourself how ridiculous they are in every respect. **Your** conscious, present day convictions must be so intense and absolute that they will create a strong enough impression on your unconscious mind to erase all the influences exerted on you by your parents, teachers and others.

We are going to use our feelings to create our life and thereby associate emotions with our desires.

4 – You are olfactive (your sense of smell)

Maybe you have seen the famous film by Dino Rossi entitled "The Perfume of a Woman". A blind man played by Victorio Gassman makes up for his lack of vision by a very strong sense of smell. He can smell fragrances and "feels" them inside. The realm of his emotions is governed by his sense of smell.

By cleverly combining the wide array of fragrances to create a new perfume, the creators of these perfumes do not aim to simply come up with a new fragrance—acidic, sweet or sour—but to provoke an emotion in the woman (or man) who buys a bottle of this perfume.

5 – You are gustative (your sense of taste)

Even if we call upon the senses of smell and taste to a lesser extent than those of sight, hearing and feelings, they can be of the utmost importance for some people.

You may be familiar with the story of the "madeleine biscuit" by the French novelist Marcel Proust. By simply dipping a biscuit in his cup of tea, the forgotten tastes of his past came flooding back into his mouth, accompanied by all the feelings he had had as a child at that time. Ask any adult why they don't like a particular dish and you will often hear the answer "because I was forced to eat it as a child". One of my friends told me that she couldn't stand fennel until one day she went shopping on the market with her boyfriend who was very surprised to learn that she didn't like this vegetable. "What? You don't like fennel!" he exclaimed, "those irresistible bulbs, full of sap and life !" In the wink of an eye, fennel had become an "irresistible bulb full of sap and life".

Since that day she has loved eating fennel. No doubt, the fact that she was very much in love with him helped her radically change her feelings towards fennel.

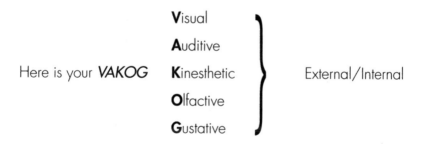

Here is your **VAKOG**

Visual
Auditive
Kinesthetic   External/Internal
Olfactive
Gustative

Each individual uses one or more predominant sensory channels and not necessarily the same ones as the rest of the family. Do you know whether your husband, your wife or your children are visual, auditive or kinesthetic?

Three of your friends come back from holiday and tell their story:

- The first: "I went to Greece this summer. Superb! The small beaches are so pretty, the sea is deep turquoise and the sky is clear blue. I visited Athens, it was beautiful".
  What is he talking about? Everything he **saw**.

- The second: "I went to the seaside this summer. We were in a holiday club. It was so noisy! Our room was above a disco. It was hell 'till 3 in the morning. We put on the air conditioning and the noise was even worse. But I really enjoyed listening to the dialect in that country". What is he talking about? Everything he **heard**.

- The third: "I went to Turkey this summer. It was SO hot! It was very relaxing. The people are very welcoming. I love the atmosphere". He is referring to his Kinesthetic channel—his **feelings**.

The words people use tell us which channel they are using at any given moment. (These are known as predicates.)

When you fall in love you don't know which channel is predominant for your partner and so you unconsciously develop all of them at the same time. This happens quite naturally.

You have a look of love in your eyes, you are careful about what you wear and about your appearance (elegant or sexy). You whisper sweet nothings, compliments…in short, words of love. You hold your partner's hand, caress his hair and skin and kiss him passionately. You choose a bewitching perfume or fragrance that suits you down to the ground and you very often go out for exquisite meals together. The whole VAKOG is satisfied.

These lovers marry and five years later what happens?

Prince charming has stopped working out and has a put on weight. He puts on his slippers when he comes home after work and it is ages since he bought and put on that delightful eau de toilette. The words of endearment have been whittled down to "darling" that has become devoid of all romantic meaning. It sounds just like when he says "Fido" to his dog (that he is also very fond of).

And the princess welcomes him home in her old track suit because it is so comfortable after a long day at work. Her hair is a mess or cut short to be more manageable. She now has trouble smelling her perfume so she puts on too much, or sometimes none at all because it's too expensive. Her soft words of love have turned into several well placed, daily yells such as "it's on the table! Come and get it! Put the lights out! It's gonna go cold!" (It certainly is). At bedtime, the beautiful, seductive princess has turned into a real sleepyhead.

This is a very good way to destroy love. Your partner will always seek the VAKOG you had at the beginning. Give it back to each other!

A visual man needs to see. He will go and look elsewhere if his wife puts out the light and then takes off her pyjamas or nightdress in bed.

An auditory woman needs to hear: "I love you darling" several times a day otherwise she will think he doesn't love her any more. Auditory people believe what they hear. Do not say things lightly.

A kinesthetic person needs caresses, kisses and tenderness. Listen to your partners and give them what they so badly need. If need be, give them the whole lot (See – Hear – Feel).

In short, to create the life you want:

- enjoy seeing what you would like to see (with your internal camera);

- listen, hear what you would like to hear, pronounce the words that you desire ;

- feel what you would feel if you had it. Over cycles of 3 – 7 – 21, (3 days, 3 weeks, 3 years or maybe 7 days, 7 weeks, 7 years, or 21 days, 21 weeks, 21 years). You live in bio-rhythms and in this way you will experience your programming exactly.

Now you are ready to program. AT LAST!

Eye movement will help us program

Your eyes are the "on/off switch" in your brain. When you move your eyes, you sweep across the zones of your brain.

Imagine yourself from behind

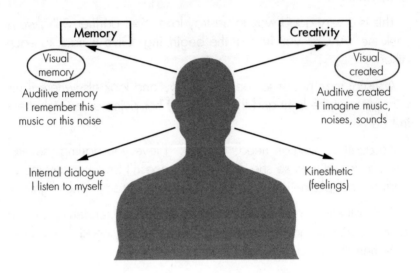

Reverse right and left if you are left handed

Ask a child to recite her lesson. You will see her eyes move upwards to the left if she is right-handed and upwards and to the left if left-handed. (This is not always a steadfast rule and can be checked with a few questions: "where did we first meet?" or "what is the colour of your mother's eyes?".) Eye movement comes before thought.

For example, it's fun to ask your friends: "what colour were the eyes of the first boy or girl you kissed in your life?" Before they answer you will see their eyes go skywards. This is known as calibrating a face. Memory is up on the left for right-handed people and up on the right for left-handers.

When I was young, a teacher once said to me: "the answer isn't written on the ceiling"...but the answer IS on the ceiling. If you don't look upwards, you don't have access to your memory which is in fact like a muscle. When we arrive in the world we have a memory potential. Small children have to continuously look upwards because their parents, the table, the TV and many other things are so much taller than they are. As adults we look down, into our feelings or into our internal dialogues.

Imagine a man who has had an accident and who has to stay in bed for several weeks. He can't use his legs as they have been plastered. When the day comes to walk again, his leg muscles will have become lifeless and he will need physiotherapy to get them moving again. It's the same for our memory.

When my father died, my mother began studying skull osteopathy. She was 65 year of age. She was worried about her memory loss and used to say: "I've got a memory like a sieve. I'll never be able to remember the names of all these little bones, ligaments, nerves or all this anatomy". So we began doing very simple mental gymnastics that took 5 minutes a day.

Try this exercise: observe a picture or painting at home, look at it very closely. Then click with your eyes up to the left (i.e. look quickly up to the left). Do this several times. Now, look closely at the painting again, then close your eyes and imagine it in your head up on the left (if you are right-handed). Open your eyes, look at the painting again and click up on the left (right-handers). The aim of this is not necessarily to help you to remember the painting but to develop the muscles of your memory in the same way as you would with weights to muscle up other parts of your body.

During the day, look upwards often. That's all. You can try this out right now and your memory will come back all by itself, more efficient than ever before.

My mother obtained her diploma of osteopathy at the age of 72. She then began studying astrology. At the age of 85 she changed her Macintosh computer for a PC. Her memory has returned and it' still there. At the age of 87 she is still surprisingly young as she has always been setting herself objectives and goals.

Let's now return to the "**on/off**" switch of this personal computer called your brain: **your eyes**.

If, for a right-hander, the memory is up to the left, then creativity is up to the right.

Therefore, to create a new program or record your desires you will need to look up or click to the right (for right-handers) and up to the left for left-handers. Exactly like a computer when you click on an icon.

Summary: what do you need if you want to create something new in your life?

- You need to know what you really want! You need to define it! We will look at this together.

- Use your senses – **see** – **hear** – **feel** – click up to the right or left to print it. Pay attention to the words you use and have fun creating attractive images of what you want. Even better than the objective itself, is to internally visualise **the consequences** these changes would have on your life if you could live out what you desire. It's as simple as that.

Memory and intelligence are not the same thing

Tell your children that memory is up to the left and that creativity is up to the right (for right-handers and the opposite for left-handers). Above all, remember that memory is not the same thing as intelligence. Learning something by heart does not prove you are intelligent. It shows you have a memory.

The pupils that used to recite that the earth was flat and that the oceans turned at the rim got full marks even though it was totally wrong.

Intelligence means creativity, inventiveness, an open mind, being able to create opportunities and effective metaphors. It also means listening and applying values such as flexibility. Arthur Vernes often used to say: "it is rare that diplomas go hand in hand with intelligence". This doesn't mean that people who are loaded with diplomas are idiots. They may have both memory and intelligence which is wonderful but not systematic.

Einstein believed that "imagination is more important than knowledge".

Some children who are considered to be poor pupils are perhaps geniuses simply unable to enter into the mould. Thomas Edison was no good at maths. Einstein was kicked out of school. The father of Conrad Black (formerly the millionaire Canadian newspaper tycoon) said to his son one day: "my great regret is having left school when I was 15. I should have left when I was 12!"

* * *

We now know how our mind works. We can use our senses and eye movement will enable us to create new programs at will. All we need to do now is change the old, unconscious mental maps our ancestors used and that we have inherited from them. This is how you are going to transform and embellish the suitcase you are carrying before passing it on to your descendents.

A summary of: "**How to create the life you want**" will then enable you to put everything into practise.

Chapter III

Meta programs

Anyone who knows how to use a computer knows how to use the mouse to click on the icons. It's the same for your unconscious mind. As soon as you open your mouth or think about something, you start using programs called meta programs.

Meta programs are the organisers of our thoughts. They are working strategies that we have in our brain which are largely outside the field of consciousness. They determine the way we behave or manage our lives as well as our reactions in the face of what we experience.

Values tell us what is important for us and in what way it is important. Meta programs tell us how to reach our goals.

You will have noticed that you do very well in some areas whereas in others you are much weaker. This is because we don't always use the same programs in all situations. It is useful to know our programs so we can make choices and change our negative tendencies.

If you become aware of your meta programs, you can choose those that will lead you to success. They can very easily be changed. All you need do is write them down, recite them, decide on this and entrust your unconscious mind with them. Cybernetics says: "We must decide often and stick to the decision".

Here are the main meta programs:

FAILURE	SUCCESS
I MUST – I HAVE TO – I OUGHT TO We can't avoid saying "I must"! You can say "we must" when it pre- supposes that you can, that you want to and you feel like it (all 3 together). If not it becomes a rigid imposed rule and the mind does not like rules.	*I WANT -* *I FEEL LIKE IT -* *I CAN* (to be able)

e.g. "I have to go and buy some bread for this evening". The presupposition is that I want some bread this evening. Or: "I have to go and get my daughter from school". You want to, it's nice for you, you can. In this case you can use "I must".

But sometimes "I must" becomes a rigid rule—"I can't do gym because I must be at home when my husband gets back". This woman thinks she can't have any activities outside the home because she has imposed this rule on herself. We could ask her: "what would happen if you weren't there when your husband got home?" "Nothing". So, go to the gym!

Another example: "the house has to be spotless every day". If you want it that way, then ok, go ahead. If not, be more flexible. It's probably not your husband who forced this on you. He would most certainly prefer to come home to more smiles and femininity than to a spotlessly clean house.

Now, it is possible to want something but not to feel like it:

e.g. "I want to do the housework but I don't feel like it". So we get "I must" do the housework". In this case, it is useful to find out what you could do to help you "feel like" doing it, to get you motivated.

If you turn tasks into fun, make them funny and even rewarding you will suddenly feel like doing them.

I explained this one day to a young woman who was complaining about having to do the housework. She complained that no-one helped her and she felt like a slave. I explained that when I was 30

I had never been skiing and that I hated the snow. One day some friends invited me to a mountain chalet for the weekend. I was cold and I kept falling down. It was much too slippery for me. I had an idea of snow that matched the conditions in which I was experiencing it.

Then my friends introduced me to moon boots. They gave me a very warm anorak, comfortable gloves, a bonnet that covered my ears, sunglasses so I could at last open my eyes wide and admire the wonderful views and surroundings. Suddenly I stopped falling over. I was now able to walk for hours with my feet firmly on the ground. I was warm all over and I began enjoying the snow.

It's the same for everything. The goal is important but you can also make the path towards it more pleasant.

Let's return to the housework. I first of all told this young woman that, above all, she should be well equipped. Thanks to all the cleaning materials on the market today, we can wipe dust away with just two fingers while we whistle. It smells nice, the dust clings to a duster that we simply throw away when we've finished. The mops almost wash all by themselves. You don't even need to bend down. And you can do all this to the music of your choice while you tone up your arm, buttock and tummy muscles as well as your thighs. Do this in five minute bursts and the housework gets done at the same time without you even having to think about it.

I explained all this to her, saying to her children: "whatever you do, don't listen coz it's so much fun that you'll all want to do the cleaning for your mum. And I want her to have some fun!" Obviously they all wanted to try it out for themselves and today they insist on doing the housework.

When you get organised and turn your chores into fun you'll see that doing the daily housework can become a need, a real pleasure.

I have always done the ironing with a cassette player in my pocket and have been able to learn a lot in this way. Otherwise I would never have had the time to study so much.

Your first meta program for success will be to turn chores into pleasure, creating pleasurable games and taking advantage of all the facilities that modern day life has to offer.

Act because you feel like it, because you want to and because you can.

①	I WANT, HENCE ... I CAN
② **Living in the past.**	I am **here and now.**
A good way to fail is to take the elements from the past and transfer them to the present. It is impossible to walk in the future whilst looking at the footprints we have just left behind us. All we can keep from the past are the teachings and benefits.	I create my own future.

I spoke earlier about the imaginary time line in your head:

N.B. you must check the goal of what you are doing. Then, stay in the here and now and ask yourself the only question possible:

"What can I do, now, to reach my goal?"

Divide what has to be done into small tasks, into small steps and it will happen.

Don't forget that your only reality is: **what you want**. Your mind has not changed the way it functions for millions of years (I know or I don't know). Don't make ambitious plans, either positive or negative. Don't expect anything, don't pre-suppose anything. Live in the present, in the experience. When a problem arises, don't link it to yourself. State it or listen to it while detaching yourself from it. Your mind will do the rest.

Your only reality is: "what you want"

② FORGET THE PAST	STAY HERE AND NOW IN THE CREATION OF THE FUTURE
③ I observe what I am MISSING. What I have not done. What remains to be done. Where I failed.	I observe what I have acquired, my potential, my qualities, my improvements and I make do with what I have. **I observe what I have already done.**

There is a word in Japanese that doesn't exist in English: kaizen: the constant improvement of my life and that of others.

Successful Japanese people make or find a daily mini-improvement to make. After 365 days this makes 365 mini-improvements that will lead to great improvements.

Let's take a schoolboy who comes home at the end of the day. His desk is a real mess. He hasn't tidied it up for weeks and he suddenly discovers a pile of homework that has to be done for the next day. Totally discouraged by the prospect of so much work he goes off to watch TV. But the schoolboy who finds a well ordered desk with room for books, who looks over what has already been studied rather than what remains to be studied, who is pleased with himself and his progress will get down to work without a second thought.

Make do with what you have. Observe what you have acquired, what you have done or obtained and you will get more and more.

	I MAKE DO WITH WHAT I HAVE, WITH MY RESOURCES. I OBSERVE MY QUALITIES AND WHAT I HAVE ALREADY DONE
④ Being in a hurry.	**Give yourself time.** I give myself time and a realistic deadline.

Let's come back to the imaginary time-line in your head. Some people are on the line and want to succeed before they have even started. They have hardly begun and they already want to see a result. To succeed you must give yourself time and a realistic deadline. Children can't be operational immediately. Be patient.

Some people open a consultancy after only 2 or 3 weeks of training. This is not realistic. Be careful when making your choices (see "The Seven Laws for Success" by Herbert Armstrong). Preparation is important in all fields, as is the learning process. Don't be in a hurry. Take your time!

A woman who weighs 265 lbs and wants to slim down to 143 lbs for her son's wedding in 6 months time won't succeed. She will say "I've failed," despite her heroic efforts. But this is not the case. Her **deadline** was not realistic.

Conclusion: aim for the skill and everything will fall into place if you are patient.

⑤ I am in an **EXTERNAL** frame of reference. I am impressionable. The last person to speak is right. I need the approval or the opinion of others.	I am in an **INTERNAL** frame of reference. **I am the one who decides.** **I know what I want.** **I make my own choices.**

A man arrives in the office in the morning and has to attend a meeting. His colleagues say to him: "You can't go and see the boss like that. Your tie is much too loud and it doesn't go with your suit". "Really! Can anyone lend me a tie?"

(External frame of reference), he changes his tie.

Another man arrives at work and his colleagues say exactly the same thing. He doesn't change his tie but goes to see the boss, self-confident and saying to himself: "they've got no taste in this place". (Internal frame of reference).

In a seminar, it doesn't take long to see which people have an external frame of reference. "Where is the lavatory please?" Someone tells them. When you watch people with an internal frame of reference, they look around at the signs and find the lavatory by themselves.

A doctor says to one of his patients: "you are seriously ill, you have … xxxxx …". "Oh no, how awful!" she replies.

This woman will experience internal psychological conflict because of the diagnosis.

If we say the same thing to a patient with an internal frame of reference we will get a different answer: "Ok. I'll have to think about that". This patient has a much greater chance of pulling through.

To create the life you want, it is essential that you become entirely responsible for your decisions, for your choices and for "how" you will go about things, in concrete terms. Do not rely on others.

⑥ I am in avoidance mode.	I am seeking the pleasure of
I am avoiding pain in the short term; the pain of doing my homework, of learning my lessons or I am avoiding the pain of doing without a nice cake (In the long term I am either useless or fat).	succeeding in the long term, of having what I want.

We can avoid dirtying our clothes or try to stay clean. In both cases, as the word is the thing (you get what you say), each person will get what they have just said, i.e. either dirty or clean clothes.

"Be careful you don't get dirty," is the perfect phrase for someone to get dirty.

Some children are in avoidance mode at school. They avoid bad grades, avoid looking ridiculous or being told off. In the long term, this is not necessarily for the best.

It is better to aim for the long term pleasure of success, to help yourself become what you wish to become. Aim for harmony, rather than trying to avoid arguments.

One can aim for values (love, harmony, justice, peace, health...) or avoid anti-values (criticism, rejection, illness, poverty). The result, of course, will be the word.

Richard Bandler has said that the mind doesn't know how to get a result but it knows how to go in a direction; values or anti-values. If you go in the direction of health, you will look young and the result will be that you have good health. The brain will not have targeted the result but you will meet it on the way. If you go in the direction of illness, you will meet it on your path with all its dreaded diseases. The mind won't have targeted this result but you will encounter it on the way (the fear of the thing creates the thing). Again, everything is a question of observation.

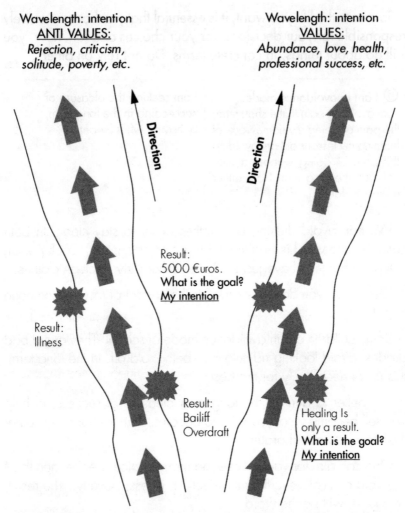

Wavelength: intention
ANTI VALUES:
Rejection, criticism, solitude, poverty, etc.

Wavelength: intention
VALUES:
Abundance, love, health, professional success, etc.

Direction

Direction

Result:
5000 €uros.
What is the goal?
My intention

Result:
Illness

Result:
Bailiff
Overdraft

Healing Is
only a result.
What is the goal?
My intention

The mind will not have targeted the result. It follows in your direction

The mind will not have targeted the result, it follows in your direction

Some women live with an alcoholic who has become violent. They cannot imagine living differently because they are in avoidance mode: they are avoiding the poverty, solitude or criticism they believe they will experience if they leave their husbands. They are not in the long term search for happiness but in avoidance of so many things. As the word is the thing, they are living exactly what they do not want to live.

One of my patients was an alcoholic. I asked him what was important to him in life. He told me that success would have been important as he wanted to be a writer but he was so afraid of being criticised and rejected that he had published nothing.

His "**criticism and reject**" anti-values were stronger than his "**success**" value. So he had turned to drink.

If I put a cake on the table, Gisèle Dupont will eat a piece whereas Claudia Schiffer will not. This is because Gisèle Dupont will avoid the pain of not having something nice in the short term whereas Claudia Schiffer will seek the pleasure of remaining beautiful in the long term.

A young man of 19 is head over heals in love with his girlfriend. He wants to go and live with her right now, to find an apartment and a little job. He is not in the long term search of giving her a comfortable life, nice surroundings and regular holidays. He is in the short term avoidance of the pain of being separated from her. Because of this he drops everything and goes to live with her without thinking of the future. In the short term he is happy but in the long term they start to argue. He has no profession and no education. They soon become short of money and finally separate.

Some young people don't like studying. They are not in the long term search for the pleasure of being interested in something or enjoying life. They are in the short term avoidance of the pain of learning and studying. This gives very poor results.

Most of the young people who have spent their adolescence in the avoidance mode live to regret it later in life when they realise that they haven't been able to build anything solid. They complain of not having the standard of living to which they aspire but they have done nothing at all to deserve it. Some of them will go back to school later on whereas others will carry on living a disorganised life with no particular goal. Others will wait for society to come to the rescue and give them everything they haven't had the courage to create and, what's more, free of charge.

It is important for students to be able to define why they want to pass their High School exams. What is their intention when they sit the exam? The exam is only a result that takes them towards a goal. The question is not to know whether a student wants to get the diploma but what he/she will do with it. "What is your intention by sitting the exam?" When this question has been answered he/she will have a much better chance of passing.

This meta-program of Avoidance/Pursuit is certainly one of the most important. Decide now to pursue the pleasure of becoming what you want to become in the long term rather than avoiding the suffering that goes with doing things you don't enjoy. Accept short term difficulties or suffering.

This should be taught in school. Wanting instant success is rarely realistic or profitable. You even have to live through a nine month pregnancy to have a child. Life belongs to those who look FAR ahead, who love what they do, do it well and stay focused on their objective.

You can turn the pain into a game, into a challenge to yourself and make the journey pleasant.

Here's a little exercise to help you move effortlessly towards the pursuit of long term pleasure. You can use it for any undesirable behaviour. A few examples: how to stop smoking, drinking or how to get children to do their homework.

If you smoke a cigarette and it's a pleasure, you are a smoker. Now, if you smoke and it makes you suffer, you can stop smoking.

If a young man believes that drugs are a real pleasure and a way to escape from his problems, he will use them. Now, if he's afraid of drugs and he associates pain with absorbing them, he will never start.

If you put pleasure or pain into what you do, you will take control of your destiny. Pleasure and pain will no longer control you, you will control them and you can put pleasure into what you choose to do and pain into what you want to abandon.

Ask yourself these questions and write down the answers:

1. "What pleasure do I associate with the act of X?" (e.g. smoking. Be honest with yourself. Think about the real pleasure that you get out of smoking).

2. "What suffering, what pain do I associate with stopping?" (e.g. stopping smoking). Write down what you are, or would be afraid of if you were to stop.

3. "What pain or severe suffering could be associated with continuing to do what I do?" (here, smoking). What is the price I will have to pay if I continue and what price am I already paying? Conjure up an internal, subjective image of yourself in your pain threshold on an imaginary screen in your head, i.e. a very painful image of the risks you are running if you change nothing. This image must make you suffer. (See the image, add the sound, hear the serious or thoroughly unpleasant remarks with a feeling of pain inside you).

4. "What intense pleasure could I put into the fact of changing?" (being a non-smoker, getting down to study and so on). This pleasure must be as strong, practical, interesting and easy as the pleasures described in N° 1 above, whilst ensuring that it eliminates the fears described in N° 2, adding personal pride and a challenge. On an imaginary screen in your head, conjure up another internal subjective image of yourself as you would be if you could get rid of this embarrassing behaviour. What would be the effects in your life if you had the behaviour you want? Make a film in your head, a precise mental image of yourself experiencing these consequences.

5. Imagine yourself in the future with your new behaviour or your new home.

Then, when you want to smoke, drink or play on the computer instead of doing your homework for example, you need only stare at a point in the room (or close your eyes) to see the first image, "suffering" and then cancel it out with the second, "pleasure" as quickly as possible. The faster you do this the faster it works. The second scenario will remain in your mind.

You will notice that, quite effortlessly, you no longer want to smoke, drink or play etc. You want to learn…in short, you now have the desired behaviour.

Champions in any field have got into the daily habit of doing what others consider to be a drag or unpleasant.

Do what you can with what you have, where you are. Always do a little more than you are doing.

	I pursue the long term pleasure of succeeding, the pleasure of becoming what I want to become.
⑦ I compare. I pursue **similarities** or resemblances.	I am **different** from others. What I do is **different**.

We can not compare one thing with another. If you go to a seminar looking for similarities, comparing it to what you already know, you might as well leave right away. You won't learn anything. You must take the information as being different.

How many parents have used this phrase: "Look at your sister or look at your brother, she/he works hard at school, she/he tidies up her/his things". What if the child answers: "well, I'm different!" And if you happen to add to that remark all the things she/he has done badly or hasn't done at all, the result is dramatic for the child.

Observe your children's qualities. Observe what they are capable of achieving and what they have done well. Things can change because your children are different from the others. They can not be the child you were at that age (in fact, the chances are that you were much worse).

We can succeed in our jobs yet make a mess of our children's education. If you compare them to other children negatively rather than recognising their strong points you risk losing the relationship. Your children are different. Make a list of all their qualities (see the meta program described above).

When a woman is fortunate enough to meet another man after a divorce, separation or bereavement, this program is essential. If she compares this man to her previous husband/partner or looks for similarities, the relationship is bound to fail. It is even worse if she spends time with him to avoid being alone rather than in pursuit of happiness. It won't be easy either if, as time goes by, she looks at all his shortcomings or at everything he is unable to do. Here is a second separation in the making (doing the same thing whilst expecting a different result is close on madness).

	Here and now everything is different.
⑧ I am **internally** connected, external frame of reference.	I am **externally** connected, internal frame of reference.

If you are "**internally connected**" you are shy, guided by your feelings and emotions. You wonder what is going to happen, how it will happen—and you would also like to do something exceptional at a particular moment. This isn't possible. You are already in the future (your mind will not follow). You listen to your internal dialogue, you frighten yourself and you influence your mind. If you add to this what you have learned, **external** frame of reference we get: the last person to speak was right, you are impressionable and you need the approval or the ideas of others. The obvious result will be stress, anxiety and the fear of being judged by others.

Now if you are "**externally connected**", you observe everything around you, you reassure people, you look after others, you notice that someone is hot or cold and you do something about it. You observe coincidences (see "The Prophet from the Andes" by James Redfield). You no longer have time to be concerned about what you feel because you are concerned about the feelings of others. You are interesting because you take an interest, you listen, you reformulate (NLP) and if you add the **internal** frame of reference, you make your own decisions in all good faith, you alone decide what is good or bad for you (which doesn't stop you listening to other peoples' point of view, or informing yourself but you don't take everything you see or read for granted).

Decide here and now to remain **externally connected/internal frame of reference. Detect opportunities. Be open and receptive.**

Shyness and a lack of self confidence

Shyness and a lack of self confidence are the result of several factors.

1. The first is a disproportionate sense of pride. That's right! Shy people want everyone to like them and respect them. This is a very good way to be unhappy because it's not possible. It is impossible to please everyone. Even well known and attractive film stars are not liked by everyone.

   Indeed, if you are criticised it means you are questionable, if you are questionable it means you have something to say, if you have something to say it means you are interesting, if you are interesting, you disturb others, if you disturb others it is proof that you exist. I prefer to exist and it is an honour to be criticised.

   The only person you need to please is yourself. I must admit that I don't necessarily like everybody and up to now no-one has died because of that. You see, it's not dangerous. Your life will already improve if you accept the simple fact that you are only loved by a certain number of people and that you can let the rest think what they want. You must want (desire) this.

   The problem disappears when you imagine you have no ego. You can speak in public without worrying about making mistakes. We stop being afraid of other peoples' judgement when we have no ego. Simplicity, the pleasure of sharing and a sense of humour are interesting values that shy people often don't have. It is essential to welcome others positively in our mind. Your self esteem will take a knock if you think people are hostile towards you (later, we will see the effect of your beliefs or predictions).

   Do the opposite. Welcoming people positively means making them seem friendly (and then they will be).

2. The second factor is that shy people use the meta program **"future"**. They create a defeatist scenario and imagine everything that has not yet happened or what they won't be able to do. Now you know how to remain in the here and now.

3. Shy people are internally connected to their feelings rather than being externally connected. They should be busy being nice to others, complimenting them on what they notice, see, hear and feel. Even people we aren't keen on will have something positive about them. Maybe they smell nice, are well dressed or are funny. We can tell them this and they will be pleased. We can also say: "It was a pleasure to meet you, I have learned a lot from you".

Shy people are not aware they are self-centred. I remember one man, a travelling salesman. He had to attend monthly meetings with other salesmen and was very uneasy about this. He said he was intimidated by them because they knew a lot more about the products and their technical aspects. He had never thought of learning from them and complimenting them on their knowledge. He could have said: "I always look forward to spending the day with you. I admire what you do, you get great results and I can learn from you". Rather than recognising the values of his colleagues and telling them so, he preferred to feel bad and complain about his own shortcomings. You see, it really takes a massive dose of pride.

4. The fourth condition to be shy is a lack of self confidence but there is no such thing as a lack of self confidence.

It is impossible to lack self confidence in everything and all the time. For example:

- A woman of 58 says to me: "I have no self confidence when I'm driving".

  Me — "does your car hold the road well?"

  Her — "no"

  Me — "have you got a wing mirror on the right?"

  Her — "no"

  Me — "where do you want to drive to?"

  Her — "to my sister's in Brittany for example"

  Me — "do you know the road well?"

  Her — "No, that's the problem. To get out of Paris I don't know the ring roads well and everyone blows their horn at me".

She's not lacking self confidence. A whole host of external factors are making her believe she has no self confidence but she's not necessarily aware of them.

We are multi-faceted personalities. Part of me wants to go to bed early whilst another wants to watch TV. Part of this woman wants to drive her car whilst another part wants security. She didn't feel at all safe and was afraid of getting lost.

We will therefore talk about improving skills rather than a lack of self confidence.

During the consultation I taught her to drive better; to put her warning lights on when she didn't know which way to go, to identify the road junctions beforehand (on a Sunday), to flash her lights when she was afraid a car would appear on her right (of course your mind doesn't know what another mind has decided to do—except for certain clairvoyants). She eventually decided to get a new car and today she is a very self-confident driver.

- An Airbus airline pilot concentrates on the control panel throughout the flight. He knows what he is doing and is in control. On final approach he asks which runway he can land on. The control tower then replies: "hold, we do not have the information..."

  This moment is very important. He cannot land as he doesn't have the information. As soon as he receives it, he will be able to land.

It is exactly the same for your unconscious mind when it doesn't have the information. **It isn't a lack of self confidence, it's a lack of knowing what, where, when and how.**

Teachers write "lacking self confidence" on children's reports. How do they know this? The child doesn't understand, period. He/she doesn't know or hasn't studied enough.

When I was a child a teacher wrote "can do better" on my report. How did she know this? Because my father was XXX and my mother YYY should I have been able to do better? I couldn't do better because I couldn't understand. We should accept that we don't know.

5. The fifth factor concerning a lack of self confidence may have its roots in a childhood trauma. In this case, as I explained in paragraph 4, you simply need to go back into the past on the time-line, to the sequence in your life that has a direct link to today's problem. This is called restructuring life's events or re-imprinting. It will provide the "broken down" child in you with the resources he/she would have needed for things to go better. The present day adult part of you will repair the child part in you. In the excellent Disney film "The Kid" that I mentioned earlier, the hero (played by

Bruce Willis) thought he was responsible for the death of his mother and didn't like his father. He relived the time when he was 8 years old and managed to make the child part of himself understand that nothing was his fault. By doing this he avoided a whole lifetime of misery. Knowledge is the liberator. Understanding the positive intentions or limits of your parents will help you to see them in a different light. You will stop being frightened and will be able to liberate the child within you.

6. The sixth factor regarding self confidence and which also gives rise to shyness is incongruence. **Congruence** means succeeding in life. What does congruent mean?

Being congruent means saying what I know, what I think, what I believe and adopting the behaviour that matches what I am. Being incongruent is just the opposite.

—"Have you seen 'Dancing with Wolves?'"

—"Oh yes, it's superb, a magnificent film."

—"Really? I haven't seen it. What's the story?"

If you haven't seen it, you are now feeling uneasy because you haven't been congruent.

Some people say what they think, what they believe but don't know. Others say what they know but don't believe it. You need all three at the same time.

I remember a friend of mine that I liked very much. She is a perfect example of congruity. We were invited to a grand hotel for the Christmas dinner of a large company. All the women were wearing evening dresses and the men were in smoking jackets. Our names had been put on the magnificently decorated table. A superb evening. My friend was in a small group opposite me looking for her place when one of the women said to another: "you have a lovely dress". The woman turned over the collar to see the brand name and replied: "yes it's Yves St Laurent. Your dress is also very nice". The pretty woman did the same and said: "yes it's by Guy Laroche". My friend then put her hand on her collar and said: "And mine is from La Redoute!". They all burst out laughing and this relaxed the atmosphere. She was always surrounded by people who loved her simplicity. Her husband, an important company director, was often involved in technical conversations. She had no problem admitting that she knew nothing about it, saying: "Personally, I didn't understand a thing. Can anyone explain?"

This gave certain people the opportunity to show what they knew and to help others who hadn't understood either, but who didn't dare admit it.

Shyness disappears when we accept that we do not know. This is much easier than pretending we know it all or that we have understood everything. What is needed here is a little simplicity and a small dose of humility.

Imagine you are dancing with someone who keeps walking on your feet. This can make you angry and you will swear never to do it again. However, if this person says: "I can't dance, I don't know how" and you reply "Come on I'll teach you", you won't mind your partner treading on your feet all evening because he/she has been congruent with you.

One day I met a young man whose parents were film stars. His godmother, a well known singer, had given him a taste for music. He had learned to play the piano by ear all by himself and played very well. After leaving school he wanted to go to a music academy to become a professional musician. After two months he was feeling totally depressed. He refused to go out, stayed in bed and had stopped playing piano. He and his family had been invited for a meal with some of my friends and they told me about this. Indeed, he refused to come to the table and stayed on the sofa. I sat down next to him and asked him a question that was close to my heart as I'd had a lot of problems learning music with a very stric father.

—"Are you any good at music theory?"

—"No! he replied."

—"So, if I've got it right, because your parents are well known and your godmother is a musician you are supposed to know all about music theory. How do you manage?"

—"That's just it! When there is sight reading to do the others do it in a few minutes. It takes me hours."

—"Have you told anyone about this?"

—"No!"

So, I then explained to him all about congruence on a piece of paper. He was totally incongruent. Behaving as if we know when we don't is unmanageable. I pointed out that the other students had learned music theory for 10 years but that he could play much better than them. "Imagine that you have several years of music theory behind you. You would be able to play any sheet music. Would you like to play at being congruent? As from tomorrow ask the teachers and the other students to help you. Tell them you're self taught, that you're no good at music theory but that you want to become a professional musician."

He did this and immediately felt much better. He realised that he had many more friends because simplicity is reassuring and that he gave others the opportunity to show what they knew by helping him out. He also recognised his own talent as a pianist.

(Meta program: observe your potential and not what is missing).

Oneday a man brought me his 24 year old son and said: "my son is lacking in self confidence when it comes to women".

"Do you know how to make love?" I asked the young man.

He blushed bright red and answered "No". He wasn't expecting this question which was, however, the only relevant one to ask.

We never lack self confidence in these 3 cases:

• When we know what we are doing.
• When we don't ask ourselves whether we will manage (future).
• When we don't ask ourselves whether people will like it.

Just do it! You can improve. Be congruent. Talk about your weaknesses and all will be forgiven. A cat that purrs and wants to be stroked doesn't ask any questions. You just accept and do it.

How long will it take a baby to catch its rattle? Quite a long time. But the baby doesn't get angry with itself because it can't do it at once. It doesn't think: "Oh what a fool I am, I can't reach this rattle". It does it over and over again until it succeeds.

Young children don't get angry with themselves when they fall off their bike. They get back on again and again until they finally find their balance. It is the same for writing. How long did it take you to learn to write all the letters of the alphabet? Children simply enter into their heads the goal they wish to reach and the mind does the rest. This shows how important it is to have a goal.

Some people have forgotten what it means to learn and want to obtain immediate results. Before doing anything successfully we must accept, for a while, that we don't know. This is the basis for any learning. We must give ourselves time and accept the learning process: **mistakes are a step on the path to success. To accept that**

we can often make mistakes and start over again is the basis of all long term success.

Give yourselves the time to become **consciously** skilled in order to become **unconsciously** skilled. When the learning process has been assimilated we then forget it and the unconscious mind does the rest.

Far too many children think it's bad to make mistakes and that they should always give the right answer. The result is that they don't dare to speak in class. Teach your children that they progress thanks to their mistakes, that their answers help everyone to understand better. Many of them live in the future. I have never seen a computer answer a question that hasn't been asked.

The difference between people who succeed and those who fail is that for those who succeed, failure doesn't exist, there are only results. Encourage your children to study their results. "How did you manage to get such a grade and what could you have done differently?" If you study the result, their grades will improve.

To do this, parents need to learn to become coaches. A coach is a trainer who takes sportsmen or women to a high level. He doesn't play the match in their place nor does he shout when the results are bad. His role is to observe what the player does well and make him/her aware of it. The coach then suggests to the player what else he/she could have done, i.e. he doesn't talk about what was bad but what could be done better (see the "sandwich technique" in the chapter: "Toolbox").

Edison didn't create the lamp bulb overnight. He failed 999 times. It was a journalist who asked: "Mr. Edison, do you intend to fail 1000 times?" "I didn't fail," he answered, "I simply discovered how not to invent the electric light bulb".

Maybe you know the story of the Japanese student who leaves school wanting to make pistons. Helped by an old friend he rents a small hangar and works day and night on his theories. Slowly but surely he makes his pistons and when he has got them right he goes off to see automobile manufacturers such as Toyota. But they tell him: "Sorry, they are too big, oversized. Go back to the drawing board". His friend says to him: "you've failed, you see". "Not at all, I've got a result", he replied.

He goes back to the drawing board and makes smaller pistons. This takes him a very long time. When he is ready to present his product to different manufacturers, war suddenly breaks out. His little hanger is destroyed along with his work. "Look, you've failed again", says his friend. "Don't ever say that", he replies "it is only a result".

So So he decides to build another workshop and asks several banks for a loan. They all say he is too young, that he has no collateral and that there is a war going on. So he goes ahead and builds his own workshop, helped by his faithful friend.

When it's finished, he works day and night on the new plans. He is soon ready and sure of himself. Just before his pistons are sold there is a bombing raid and his workshop is entirely destroyed again. He has lost everything. His friend leaves him at this point but for him it is still only a result.

He is alone and walks around the ruins of his village with his hands in his pockets. He notices cans of petrol that the Americans have left there. "This is a gift from the Americans," he thinks to himself. He collects all the cans and stores them in a field whilst trying to decide what to do with them. Then (dance with the unconscious) he suddenly has the idea of making small engines for the bicycles of the people from his village who had lost everything. He did this but he was told that they were too big, they backfired and smelt awful.

Then he suddenly had a brilliant idea; he would give the children of the baby-boom personal transportation. This was to become a great success in Japan and in the USA and he became a millionaire.

This is the story of Mr. Honda who never failed but only got results. He gave himself time. He used what was at his disposal (without looking at what was missing). He was trying to achieve something long term. He remained externally connected, observing his needs, with an internal frame of reference. He never let himself be influenced by his friend and held fast.

All the meta programs are excellent. You will understand later with "The Seven Rules for Success" by Herbert Armstrong that he was able to adapt and get around his results. Well done Mr. Honda!

7. The last parameter regarding a lack of self confidence is that of giving other people too much importance. Look differently at someone you consider to be important. Imagine him/her with a clown's nose or Mickey Mouse ears. Make the image smaller. You can also imagine them with no clothes on, imagine the flaws (I won't say what, let your sense of humour run free) and smile.

There is no such thing as a lack of self confidence

- Learn to communicate. Be externally connected, observe and reformulate what people say to you (see "active listening" in the chapter on "Tools"). Welcome people positively in your head.
- Stay in the here and now without wanting to do something exceptional at a particular time.
- Accept that you make mistakes and that you can't please everyone. Be congruent. Improve your skills, accept that you don't know.
- Be in harmony with your values and not those of other people. Feel right in what you do and give yourself reasonable deadlines to reach.
- Learn to adapt your behaviour to the context. The same behaviour will not produce the same results in all contexts. Be flexible (see "the Behaviour Generator" in the chapter on "Tools").

A Summary of meta programs: clearly defining your objectives will make all the difference to your success.

- Wanting to, saying: **"I really want to"** (where there's a will there's a way). I can if I want.
- I give myself **time** and a **realistic deadline** to succeed in whatever I do.
- I am in an **internal frame of reference.** I'm the one who wants. I'm the one who decides. I'm responsible and I rely on myself.
- **I connect myself externally**: what I do is useful to others. I make my contribution and help to improve the life of each individual. I pay attention to others.
- **I pursue long term success,** I am aiming to…
- I observe a mini-improvement to my qualities and potential every day. "I'm getting better every day in all respects", is a famous saying by the French writer Emile Coué[1].
- You influence your mind because it doesn't know what is true or false. You have understood that it will follow your observations and improve your life in quality and potential.
- **I make do with what I have.** By aiming for my goal and observing what I have already accomplished, my mind will provide me with more and more possibilities.

---

1 "Conscious autosuggestion according to Emile Coué", published by Quintessence.

- **I am in the here and now,** creating the future. As Bruce Lee said: "to live here and now we must learn the art of dying, dying with regard to everything that belonged to yesterday".
- I am different from other people. I have my style and my life will be different.

Other meta programs are important.

GLOBAL   or   *SPECIFIC*

To create the life you want, it is best to be precise (specific) and to define what you want in detail. At the outset, you can look at the overall picture and then learn to enter into precisely what you want and the precise action required.

OPTION   *PROCÉDURE*
                       or
Improvise   *Have a plan*

It is important to know how to improvise when necessary and to have a plan of action so you can act in a concrete manner. You can't build a house without a plan. In the chapter "Abundance" you will see how important it is to have a plan of what you need so that your conscious mind can provide it.
Make plans!

Write down the list of meta programs for success and read them aloud once. Entrust your unconscious mind with them and it will do the rest. **You can decide to do this now.**

Enjoy playing with your unconscious mind and it will send you ideas and solutions. As soon as it has understood what you want, it will give you the means to accomplish it. Act in the order that things come to mind.

Now that you know your five senses, the movement of the eyes and the appropriate meta programs, you are getting close to success. You now need to learn to define your objectives, those that will lead you to success in your new life.

Let us turn the page...a very appropriate expression here!

CHAPTER IV

FIXING OBJECTIVES
AND KNOWING HOW TO REACH THEM

This is your key to success. It would be very useful to know how you sometimes managed not to reach your goals so that from now on you can learn how to follow your plans through to the end.

Before developing the easy-to-apply, logical reasoning of your mind, we can mathematically check out whether it works using the theories of the epistemologist Karl Popper ("Objective knowledge" published by Oxford University Press). His theory of three worlds can be understood like this:

- **World 1** – the physical world. I receive images (external visual) or I create images (internal visual). I feel an emotion in both cases. I hear what is going on around me (external auditory) or I argue, I have an internal dialogue (internal auditory). The words I pronounce conjure up an image and provoke a feeling (kinesthetic); external feelings (on the skin) and internal ones (emotion). All this is the physical world.
- **World 2** – The mind is impregnated with all this (from what you say and from your images).
- **World 3** – The mind looks for solutions (the world that the human mind has created in general. World 3 is autonomous. We can make theoretical discoveries in the same way we can make geographical ones. This world is infinite, insatiable and unachievable, as far as human beings are concerned). Your mind seeks solutions ad infinitum **that will descend into the physical world.**

World 3	– Solutions that return to the physical world
World 2	– The mind is impregnated with this
World 1	– Physical–Images–Sounds (words)–Feelings

Worlds 1 and 3 can only interact with each other via World 2, with which they are both interacting (argumentation, images, feelings — impregnation — solutions).

This simply means that when you pronounce words and sentences, your mind creates images that inevitably trigger an emotion, a feeling. After impregnation[1], it looks for solutions that will reach you very quickly in the physical world.

Do not intellectualise what you read. Simply practise it on a daily basis and be careful how you formulate things. As soon as you have expressed a desire and created an emotion, the solution will come to you. It is the same for the things you do not want, the solution will also come to you and you will think you are unlucky.

Close your eyes or stare at a point in the room. Now, create an image in your mind, i.e. an internal representation of what you desire and create an emotion (enjoy feeling what you would feel if you already had it. Keep hold of this feeling). Assert that it is legitimate and state: "when I've got it, as soon as…"

Above all, do not look for a solution, simply enjoy the image. The solution will arrive in a roundabout manner and it will seem so easy! (Of course, as we will see later, your objective must be realistic.)

For example, one evening I was in my office wondering how I was going to fit a bookcase I needed and a table for coffee breaks into my empty corridor. It was late and I began staring at a point in the room. With my internal movie camera I was able to see my private apartment and a very cluttered bedroom on a giant screen. I moved out the unused table and the bookcase that took up too much space. The room suddenly became spacious and usable. I then shifted my gaze and went back to the internal image of the empty corridor of

---

1 Impregnation means: like a sponge that absorbs water on a table. It is this fast!

my office. Presto! I put the table and the book case in there. It was like being Mary Poppins or "Bewitched".

I then said aloud: "when this furniture has been put in, it will be more pleasant and convenient for everyone". I was delighted, (I created the emotion that went with the idea of this new layout). It was so simple. Now I could go home.

The next day a friend phoned and said : "I'm in Paris, do you need anything doing?" "Oh yes", I said "could you go and pick up a bookcase and a table?" It all went so smoothly. How was that possible?

Last year I wanted to take my grandson on holiday to a very quiet place with a private swimming pool. The problem was that little Guillaume sleeps until 5 p.m. and his brother Kevin gets impatient for his little brother to wake up so he can go swimming. I wanted him to be able to come and go freely without having to wait. What's more I had to take a nanny who would do the cooking because I wanted to finish the book I was writing. All that seemed rather complicated. I visited several travel agents but I had left it late and everything was already booked up. So I decided to write down precisely what I wanted and I created an internal image of a beautiful place. I could see myself at a table beside a swimming pool, someone had done the cooking for me and I argued the advantages of this situation. I was delighted and excited. That was all I needed to do.

In July, three weeks before my holidays were due to start, my son gave me some news of my ex brother-in-law. I hadn't heard from him for ages. My son said he often mentioned me and would have loved to see me again. Out of curiosity I called him right away. He told me he was retired and that he had renovated a farm with a lovely swimming pool. He told me he grew his own vegetables and ate only what he produced. He had chickens, good eggs and everything was organic. So he invited me to stay. This was the best holiday I had had for years. I had an office with a beautiful view where I could write and this funny and charming man cooked both lunch and dinner for us all. He taught my grandson how to garden and pick vegetables, he even had a horse. Everything was much better than I had imagined. All my criteria had come together as if by magic and we had all our meals beside the pool.

I could give you thousands of examples like this. Chance does not exist. What happened can be demonstrated and reproduced by you. Some people naturally use the technique of goal determination below. They perfectly enter into the theory related to the theory of the three worlds, the mathematical law.

If and if only if–as if = it is

(This is a mathematical law: a necessary and sufficient condition for something…)

What does **as if = it is** mean?

Well, if you act as if, as far as your mind is concerned, it is. Act **as if** you were ill and you will become ill. Act as if you were angry and you will become angry.

> "Kneel, pray and you will believe." Pascal.

Act as if you were unlucky and you certainly won't have much luck.

When I was a child I was very frightened of storms. I was so afraid that I had panic attacks. I would get into my parents' bed and my father would tell me a story. This may have looked like a strategy to have this privilege but when I grew up I was still as afraid of storms.

Later on when my son Sebastian was two, I was alone in a large house in Provence in the south of France. Around 6 p.m. a storm broke out and storms are much more frightening in Provence than they are in Paris. All of a sudden everything went black as if night had fallen. After a bright and powerful fork of lightening there was an enormous clap of thunder. I felt my panic reaction coming on and Sebastian began to cry. I said to myself: "I can't let my son see that I'm frightened". So I pretended to be calm and collected. I acted "as if". I took him by the hand and led him to the window where we waited for another bolt of lightening. The next one was even brighter than the others. It had been very hot all day and the rain now began cooling the air. I said to Sebastian: "Oh look how lovely it is! All the sky is lit up and the flowers are so pleased to have some rain on them". When the thunder had passed I told him that it was Father Christmas playing bowls with the angels. "Can you hear? They are running around looking for the balls and it echoes everywhere".

Twenty minutes later when the storm was over I realised that I hadn't been afraid and since then I have never been frightened of storms.

As if = it is

Maxie Maulsby, who has studied beliefs all his life, said that change is immediate but people do not believe it for two reasons. First of all, because they would become responsible for their own lives, for their emotions and for what they have done and secondly because they prefer to die rather than believe they were wrong. But you have never been wrong. You acted with your childhood filters, with your tools, your beliefs. Today you can have other beliefs, other tools and other strategies.

Imagine you are going to see a play. You are sitting in the theatre where you can see and hear from a certain angle. At the interval, as there are free seats on the other side of the room you change places. Now you see and hear from a different angle. Does this mean you were wrong to sit where you sat in the first place? Of course not, it simply means that you are having another experience, it's different.

I have experienced and lived immediate change. When I was young I was very sensitive and blushed easily. I had been afraid of my father throughout my childhood. It didn't take much for my legs to feel like cotton and for me to go to pieces. When I got married I looked sure of myself but was I still just as sensitive. One day when I was 8 months pregnant I caught a train at Vigneux-sur-Seine station in the outskirts of Paris. When I tried to obliterate my ticket on the platform, try as I may, the machine wouldn't work. As I didn't have much time to spare I decided to get on the train anyway. Thirty years ago there was only one inspector per train and when he found people cheating he took them to his office in the main station in Paris. Obviously, that day I was caught with a non-obliterated ticket. I explained about the machine that wouldn't work and the fact that I was pregnant in the hope of some leniency but to no avail. He said it was as if I had no ticket at all. He was also into the "as if". I had the impression that everyone was looking at me and I was as red as a beetroot, petrified. On arriving in the station, I followed him to a large room. My legs were numb. On a big, empty desk there was a telephone and a sheet of paper. The inspector went off to get the papers he needed to give me a fine and while I was waiting I gazed at the desk and the paper. On it was written: "Memo; the obliterating machine in Vigneux-sur-Seine is out of order". When he came back I said to him: "Look at this memo. Now I want your name and number!" I don't know whether it was my baby that suddenly gave me the strength but in that instant I swore that never again would I be influenced by anything. I forbid myself to go to pieces in the future whatever the circumstances and promised to be myself at all times. It only took me a few seconds. I left that office as I am today; happy with myself, proud and self confident.

Your unconscious mind understands this very well. Swearing to yourself, promising yourself and forbidding yourself things will bring an immediate result. But you must decide this.

When you have defined your objective, do "as if" you had already reached it. How would you behave if you had what you wanted? Do "as if", adopt the attitude. Because if, and if only if, you do as if = It is. If you do not act "as if", nothing will happen.

Totally by chance, (chance does not exist) when I went home early one evening, I watched an episode of the TV series "Who's the Boss" and my attention was caught by a short passage. Angela works in advertising. As she is divorced she lives with her son Jonathan and her mother. She has a good salary and standard of living. Mona, her mother says she should take on a housemaid. Angela finally decides to employ someone but chooses a man who turns out to have a little daughter called Samantha. They all get on well together and we want to see something develop between Tony and Angela. One day Tony persuades her to go on holiday for two weeks with the whole family. During the holidays a very important meeting takes place in Angela's company. Her colleagues try to get in touch with her to get her to come back to the office but to no avail. Tony manages to hide all the messages they send her. When she returns to work she is fired. At first she is worried and telephones everyone she knows to try to find another job. She soon discovers that when you are in trouble friends are few and far between. Tony says she could sell her Jaguar and he offers to work for her without pay for a few weeks.

Angela thinks for a few seconds, picks up her handbag, puts on her coat saying "I'm going shopping for a fur coat".

"What?" says Tony, "I just offered to work for nothing and you're going out to buy a fur coat?"

"If you act like you're poor", says Angela, "then you will be poor; if you act like you're rich then you'll be rich".

This perfectly fits the formula: AS IF = IT IS.

How many people watching this episode of "Who's the Boss" actually remembered or gave a second thought to this extract? For the mind, simulation is exactly the same. How long have you been behaving as if you were unlucky or fed up? Through this law we find the three worlds of Popper that I described above.

The five laws of the mind

- First law – the law of REPRESENTATION. This is the image created by our internal movie camera, the subjective internal representations.
- Second law – the law of OPTIMISATION. These are the words we use, our arguments.
- We find Popper's World 1 in these two laws; the physical world.
- Third law – the law of IMPREGNATION (World 2 of Popper). The mind is impregnated with the images and words it receives (it absorbs them like a sponge).
- Fourth law – the law of EXACTITUDE. The world of solutions (World 3 of Popper): the mind cannot be mistaken. It looks for solutions. Imagine you are on the edge of the pavement, you start crossing the road but you didn't notice an oncoming lorry. Your brain will make you jump one step backwards. You will say "it's a reflex". It is quite simply a spatio-temporal operation performed by your brain that was not mistaken. It could have made you move forwards and you would have been sucked under the lorry. Your brain is constantly doing mathematical, spatio-temporal calculations. In this fourth law, the solutions are countless (unfathomable World).
- Fifth law – the outcome.

What you are experiencing today is the outcome, the solution your mind has found (in 4), after impregnation (in 3) following your arguments and images (in 1 and 2). It would be a pity to intellectualise it. Live it, practise it and do it at least once with a simple subject.

My partner, Thierry, wanted to fit a kitchen for me but died before being able to do so. I kept the plans. My kitchen was becoming increasingly outdated so one day I decided to have it all changed. I got out the plans and went off to see a number of specialist shops to choose the colour of the units and the tiles. I decided on yellow and blue and on a particular model of kitchen. I was able to visualise exactly what I wanted and I used the arguments: "When, as soon as...etc". What's more, I created the emotion linked to this change (the first two laws had been satisfied: see, hear and feel). I also respected the key elements when determining an objective: Precise, Realistic, Responsible, Ecological and Measurable (I set myself a realistic deadline of one year saying to myself: "In exactly one year I'll be in my new kitchen"). And then put the sheet of paper back on the shelf. The only detail that my friends found unrealistic was the price. I didn't want to spend more than 4000 $ (2500 £). Given the plans, this sounded unrealistic.

But we mustn't forget the power of the unconscious mind. There is no such thing as difficult or easy as far as the mind is concerned. After visualising, representing and arguing, my mind was impregnated and began looking for solutions without my even realising it. Two months later during one of my workshops in Paris, one of the participants Jean Jacques said to me "your workshops are great and I'd love to come to all of them but it's so expensive for me". I knew a little about him. He was a kitchen specialist but wanted to change jobs. I asked him if he still had special rates at suppliers. "Of course", he answered. "Ok. How about coming to all my workshops free of charge if you put in a kitchen for me that I buy using your special rates?" He agreed and did everything, including the plumbing and the electricity. Today I have a beautiful, fully fitted kitchen that only cost me 3500 $ (2200 £). Isn't that wonderful? I could give you hundreds of examples like this.

I hope you are now feeling frightened when you think back on the way you speak to your family or to yourself, on the conscious or unconscious way you have of creating images, because the result happens to you all by itself.

It is now your turn to argue for anything you want. Your life is in your own hands or rather in your own thoughts. For your brain, there is what you want and what you do not want. It is not logical to cling to something we don't want.

Your perception of things is automatic. The world you live in, as well as what your body experiences, is determined by the way you have learned to perceive it. If you change your perception you inevitably change your world.

You can live in a cruel and hostile world. If you are on a different wavelength, you will meet and spend time with different people who are on your frequency.

If you adopt a positive, inquisitive, aware, audacious and loving attitude, your world will start to look like what you want it to be.

Although each individual seems distinct and independent, we are all connected at levels of intelligence that govern the entire cosmos. Our mind is one aspect of a universal spirit.

We are never alone.

If you put complete trust in this process, answers and solutions will come to you via an intelligence that is infinitely vaster than your conscious spirit, (dancing with one's unconscious mind means letting things happen).

You simply need to let go, entrust your unconscious mind with your problem and leave the time necessary for things to happen by themselves.

Energy always answers your expectations. The information you need concerning the "what and how" will come to you at the right moment. You will also meet the right people. Information is a permanent flow that you are constantly filtering depending on your needs (see chapter on "How to Recognise Synchronicities"). You mind selects what you need to know.

Obviously, the closer you get to a higher level of vibration, i.e. the more you think positively, the faster the messages will arrive.

Things will come to you if you use your talents, creativity and skills with a beneficial and positive intention. If you want to perpetuate your actions, you will have to act in a win/win context (good for you, good for others) in your best interests and in those of others (see the "Laws of Abundance").

If you cannot feel this current, change your objectives until they point in a direction that will lead you back onto your path.

In one day, you can expect to meet people who will unknowingly give you the messages you need to do what you want. If you can sharpen your awareness to this phenomenon, it will happen. Of course, if you accustom your conscience to the opposite, i.e. to doubt, then nothing will happen or you will get what you do not want.

When you want to develop positive energy, it is impossible for you to fail because in the field of subtle interaction: WANTING MEANS ACTING AND WANTING MEANS BEING ABLE.

The necessary condition for success is the awareness that success is within your reach.

Don't waste your time imagining punishment for people who have offended you in any way. You will connect to the same wavelength as a righter of wrongs. It is much better to connect to the creation of your own life and the scenario you want. Let go of the past, let go and you will win out in the long run. The new context will be better and better, (we will see this in the chapter on "Abundance").

Now, wanting something implies that we don't have it. When will you stop wanting it? When you have obtained it. Maybe one day you were hoping to meet your soul mate during your holidays. So, you dressed nicely, you put make-up or perfume on, you kept your eyes peeled, you smiled, you stayed alert to everything around you but nothing happened. The holiday was coming to an end and you said to yourself: "it's too late, no luck this time". So you gave up. You started packing your cases and thinking about what lay ahead. You went out for one last walk badly dressed, unprepared and lo and behold, you met someone!

Have you ever tried to remember someone's name? The more you try the less you remember. The more you want to find it, the more distant and blurred it becomes. So you stop trying. A few seconds or minutes later you say "ah, found it, he was called so and so". This is what letting go means.

"**Wanting**" creates stress and when you get what you want the stress increases because you are afraid of losing it. Stop wanting things, especially for others (even your family). Simply define your desires, create a clear image of them, entrust your unconscious mind with them and let go, whilst respecting the laws of the mind.

This detail is of the utmost importance to create the life you want. Your unconscious mind reasons, with a logic of its own. Your objectives must meet certain criteria: they must be precise, realistic, responsible, ecological and measurable. Let's look at this more closely.

Above all, when you have a desire, do not give your mind the solution. Do not tell it how to do it or what it must do. If you do, it will let you sort it out by yourself. It is up to the mind to answer the "where, how, with who or with what" questions.

As I've said before, act as if you had succeeded. Don't wait to feel good before behaving as if you feel good. On the contrary, behave as if you feel good in order to feel good, (act like a winner to be a winner). Your mind will always believe in the behaviour you have set up (see "Behaviour Generator" in the chapter on Tools).

The following is one of the major keys to success.

How to determine an objective and clarify your goals to make them accessible and feasible

The logical reasoning of your unconscious mind

Now you are aware of the power of your thought and of the speed at which you create, you are ready to learn how to create the life you want in a rational way.

We owe this very simple way of understanding how the mind reaches an objective, to John Grinder (professor of linguistics) and Richard Bandler, a mathematician. They are the founders of NLP.

Your mind follows the same process whether it is a simple desire or a more complicated project. You are sure to succeed if you respect the following points that the mind covers in a few seconds. If you forget one of the parameters, your objective will remain blurred and therefore inaccessible.

In NLP this is called a **PREM**[1] and in the anecdotes I have given you above, it's clear that the result has nothing to do with magic.

It is possible to pursue several objectives at the same time but you should make a PREM for each of them. Each objective should be carefully laid out on a dedicated page. You will recognize the meta program "be specific". Let's begin.

Select a project or desire that you particularly want to fulfil. Write it down in terms of "what you want". Take care not to confuse the path and the outcome, e.g. wanting to move house is a path, moving into bigger accommodation is an outcome. Wanting to lose weight is a path, weighing 110 lbs is an outcome. How do we refine and clarify the real goal in a natural manner? There is simply the objective and the intention.

1. **Define and entrust your mind with the advantage of getting what you want or the advantage of reaching your objective.**

   Children who can't see the point of learning biology because they will never use it when they are older will not learn. If, however, they

---

1 Precise, Realistic–Responsible, Ecological and Measurable.

say to themselves that they don't know what they'll do when they are older and that it may be of use to them, then they will learn.

I couldn't understand why my father made me do so many things. Every Thursday (which was the day off school in those days) he took me to learn shorthand. I saw no use in this at all. How could he know that 20 years later I would be able to attend important seminars and conferences and, thanks to my 210 words a minute, be able to take notes almost as quickly as the spoken word, whereas the other participants came along with cassette recorders that they would never have time to listen to again. My father followed his intuition. He thought about the future and was able to heed the messages from his unconscious.

People who look far ahead of them are good drivers. Teach your children to dream their future and arouse their interest so they will come into contact with all sorts of things: music, science, sowing, painting, sculpture, sport, dancing, DIY and so on. Project future **intentions**. Look far ahead for yourselves and for them. The more you learn, the more your brain develops what it needs in order to learn and this is true at any age. Saturation is impossible for your unconscious mind and its 28 billion cells/computers.

I asked my sons to choose a musical instrument. Benoit chose the saxophone but saw no point in playing when he was young. Every Wednesday, (the day off school), he would sing the song he had composed to complain: "mummy, I don't want to go". But for his 18th birthday we had a party with his friends. All of them were envious when Benoit started playing the saxophone and he later said to me: "when I think that I almost stopped playing the saxophone…it makes me shiver".

Music is a part of his life just as it has been a part of mine. I expressed my first broken heart with my guitar and, as a child I didn't know just how important music would become later on in my life. Your unconscious mind knows your future. Follow your intuitions and trust your unconscious mind.

The starting point of any plan is the ability to see the point. When you want to reach an objective, nothing will happen until your unconscious mind has understood the point of it. I recently asked a young, paralysed woman what advantages she could see in walking: "I don't really know," she said. "I'm very well organised, I have a car and friends."

I didn't need to ask her anything else. She had already given me sufficient reason for her not to walk again. It would have been no use trying to help her.

At school, the number of children who see no point in what they do is way too large. The teaching profession is in need of tools and techniques to bring about great change. We could start by not frightening children by telling them how awful life will be if they don't work hard or by belittling them. These techniques are similar to those used in coaching. Parents are also coaches (trainers) for their children. I told you that a trainer doesn't play the match in the place of the sportsman/woman. He is there to create the motivation and the will to continue, (see the "sandwich" technique in "Toolbox").

The right questions in this case are:

- What would be the point in my doing X? or: if there was a point what would it be, compared to what I have today?
- What would I get out of it that I don't have today?
- What advantages would I get out of it?

Answer these questions before carrying on.

2. **Don't be afraid of losing something by reaching your objective. Any change is frightening or awakens fears.**

A woman who is afraid of losing her independence by getting married won't meet anyone. If she wants to have a happily married life she can put in place a plan to meet a man who will let her be free to act, to learn and who will let her remain independent. As soon as her fears have been replaced by certainty and efficient solutions, life can go on.

One of my friends wanted to start a business with a childhood friend called Alexander. He saw some great advantages in this such as being able to trust him completely. But when I asked him: "If you were to have any reservations about working with Alexander what would they be?"

"I'd be afraid of falling out with him and spoiling a good friendship," he replied.

It is when we become aware of our fears that we can then get rid of thembecause:

A problem = a solution

The word solution would not exist if the word problem did not also exist.

Sometimes a "good" psychotherapist can be useful. I say a "good" psychotherapist because talking for hours "in" the problem with no precise tools to solve it is of no real use. Indeed, a good psychotherapist doesn't try to tell the patient what he/she would do in their position but helps them find their own solutions that match his/her model of the world.

So I said to this friend: "if I gave you efficient communication techniques to help you reply elegantly when you disagree and if you were positive that your friendship couldn't be shaken would your business plan still be valid?" "Yes, of course it would," he replied.

Solutions need to be efficient, practical, easy to implement and isomorphic, (i.e. they adhere point by point to the subject and the life of the person in question).

We discover that multiple solutions exist in all cases. As soon as your unconscious mind has been impregnated with your intentions, a creative part of you goes to work and you will encounter a whole range of opportunities. This is why it is vital that you know how to ask yourself the right questions.

Fears can be of two kinds: those linked to the objective itself and those encountered in the process set up to reach it.

For example, if you ask an obese woman what she has to fear by becoming slim she will obviously answer: "nothing at all. It's a dream, it would be wonderful". Hence, no fear.

But: "what might you be afraid of in the slimming process?" Here, she may well be afraid of it being complicated, rigid, draconian, painful or boring and this will explain why she has not, as yet, entered into the process.

"If I gave you the absolute certainty that you could lose weight without a diet, easily whilst eating tasty and pleasant food, would you be motivated by your objective?" Of course. But you still need to know how to do it (this is the subject of my next book: "Obesity – overweight and cellulite").

Check here and now that you are not afraid of losing anything by reaching your objective. Otherwise, find some solutions before carrying on. **How can you do this?** Simply by updating your fears and by sweeping them away during the following process.

- What would be the point of doing XX?– What would I get out of it that I don't have today?
- If I was afraid of something, what would it be? Or: if there was something to be afraid of what would it be?
- What is missing that I don't have and that is preventing me from reaching my objective?

By studying these questions you will become certain you can succeed or become aware that you already have everything it takes to succeed.

You now need to refine your objective and here is how your unconscious mind reasons:

There is the **present state** and the **desired state**.

Present State

Have you ever noticed how much time you spend talking about a problem without ever having envisaged a desired state (what you would like in its place). Ideally, you should spend 5% of the time on the problem and 95% on the solution (the unconscious mind will find it).

You will be able to clearly define your objective if you study the present state. And it is valid even if you are buying a washing machine.

Present state: how many people does it have to wash for? What will I get out of it that I don't already have? What are the drawbacks of the machine I have? What is the problem and why is it a problem? We can't define real needs before we have understood the limits of the here and now.

The present state also studies the passive, i.e. the way in which you experience something and how it helps you change your strategy. Because people who repeatedly do the same thing whilst expecting a different result will have to wait a long time (think about this the next time you form a new relationship/couple).

The right questions:

What is my life today?

What do I want to change?

What is the problem and in what way is it a problem?

The desired state

This is the objective you stated above, your desire, your project.

Check it is expressed in a way that says what you really want and not what you don't want because the "word is the thing". You must also be able to **visualise it**.

Fixing an objective such as "being happy" is much too vague.

In the case of a breast cancer, for example, don't say: "I want to get better", say "I want my left breast to be as healthy as my right breast". For a skin problem: "I want clear, soft and healthy skin". **The image will be associated with the objective expressed.** As your unconscious mind now knows your intentions and the advantages to be gained, the image will come all by itself. You have already gone a long way towards determining your project.

Here are the four parameters you will need to respect if you want to succeed and they will make all the difference: **PREM**.

*An objective can only be **personal**. You cannot have an objective for someone else. No computer can solve the problem of another computer. Parents can not want anything for their children. All they can do is to arouse an interest for many different subjects. Children must have their own objectives.*

First parameter: "Precise"

Write: "I want to be able to visualise...xxxx".

We will now narrow down your intentions and clarify the objective.

You will need to ask yourself the question concerning your intention twice.

Example: "I want to move house"

- What is my intention in wanting to move house? "To move into a bigger house!" (I already have an image).
- What is my intention in wanting to move into a bigger house? "To give my family more space and comfort". This is the real goal. Only now can a multitude of means appear, not only to help you move into a bigger house but to provide the family with more comfort.

Another example: "I want to lose weight"

- What is my intention in wanting to lose weight? "to weigh 110 lbs".
- What is my intention in wanting to weigh 110 lbs? "to like myself and be able to wear what I want". This is the real goal and only now can things be possible (and be visualised).

  Wanting to lose weight doesn't conjure up the image of the real goal or being able to lose weight, so the solution is to stay fat. Under these conditions you will remain in the same state.

The reason why you have sometimes not reached your objectives is that your unconscious mind has not understood the real intention and the image was not the one you wanted.

a. The intention of the intention is the goal.

As you have seen in the previous paragraph, if you don't know the goal of what you are doing then there is not much point in doing it. Indeed, very often, if some people were to ask themselves the question: "what is the goal of saying what I'm saying?" When they realise that their goal is not necessarily timely, useful or nice they would soon stop.

Your goal should be win/win (good for you, good for others). If you want to open a restaurant your intention is not to make money but to please your customers. In this way you will earn money.

Take a woman who says: "I'd like to have a baby". Ok, what is the goal?" "I'd feel more like a woman and it could bring my husband and I closer together". And what about the child?

So my intention, my goal is...

b. What will it bring me? In what way is it important for me?

You will find the advantages studied above plus the values that they represent for you (serenity, peace, love, self-fulfilment).

"What is important for me in terms of values, in the fact of doing...or having...on top of the advantages already mentioned?"

You are looking for values: "Love, harmony, independence, creativity, success, freedom..." Values are what make you act. They are located at a very high level of thought (in the chapter on "Tools", look at how to develop a value by yourself and make a success of your life).

It is impossible to get anything going without having a value to motivate you. Here is an example: I asked someone who has managed to stop smoking: "Why is it important for you to be a non-smoker? What do you get out of it that is important for you?"

The answer: "health, beauty, I want to stay young. Respect for the environment, personal pride and freedom".

There is no shortage of values there!

I asked someone who hasn't managed to give up smoking the same question: "my wife would be pleased, or...the doctor told me to stop, or...so I won't get ill".

This person is not pursuing a value but is avoiding an anti-value and, what's more, he is in an external frame of reference.

I once asked a good student: "what is important for you about being good at school? What do you get out of it that is very important for you?"

He told me: "I want to have a good place in society when I get older, to succeed both professionally and socially. I want to have money, to be free and independent, enjoy what I do and fulfil my aims".

There are a good many values in that sentence. I asked a dunce the same question: "No idea!" came the answer. No values there.

We are motivated by the image of our goal and the values that encourage us to act. High school would be so much more interesting with this type of program! So many teenagers have neither an intention nor an image of any goal and are totally unaware of any values.

We are still "being precise". For example: what do you have to do to lose weight, to weigh 110 pounds, to like yourself and wear what you want?

Present state: I am X feet tall and I weigh X pounds

Desired state: I want to weigh 110 pounds

Then, and to associate the image with the desire: "who do you want to look like?"

Look through a magazine and cut out the picture of someone you want to look like. Stick a photo of your face on the face in the picture. Things are now starting to become precise. If you use a photograph of yourself when you were slim, this is a picture "of the past". Your mind will think: "that's me when I was slimmer". Here and now, give your mind the image of what will be created in the future.

Put this picture in or on your bedside table. You don't even have to look at it. Your unconscious mind will see it. The only thing you need to do when you put it somewhere is to think "PREM", without making any comment. You will know how to do this by the time we have finished this demonstration: (what I want is precise—it is realistic. If other people are slim why can't I be too? It is responsible. I'm the one who wants it. It is ecological, I entirely agree with it. It is measurable, I give myself one year. In one year, to this day, I will weigh 110 pounds).

If you want to meet the love of your life, find the ideal job or the perfect place to live (use the expression "place to live" because if you say apartment or house you will influence your mind. Let your mind find what suits you best because it knows what is good or bad for you much better than you do).

Above all, do not influence your unconscious mind with requests and answers. Let it look for you. Do not do anything more than consciously define exactly what you want in terms of criteria.

When you play "bowls" (petanque) you don't consciously know the exact distance between your feet and the jack ball. But your unconscious mind does. Some players get prepared, start calculating, make everyone stop talking, blow on the ball, move their arms about, throw and...miss! My son is very good at "bowls". When it's not his turn he chats and his mind is elsewhere. "Benoit, it's your turn," we tell him. He comes over and asks: "where is the jack ball?" "Over there". He looks, takes his ball and throws...exactly in the right place. This is very frustrating for some people but it is the best way to succeed. Your unconscious mind knows how to aim straight but you can't do this consciously. Benoit's asset is that he doesn't think or reason (when he is playing bowls of course).

When you want to go from one place to another you simply decide to go. Your mind does the rest and you arrive right on target. As I mentioned in the previous paragraph, you don't consciously think "I have to lift my leg, bend my knee, stretch out my foot, put it on the floor and so on". The same goes for the other leg otherwise you will fall flat on your face.

I once worked with a gifted golfer. He was a really talented player and won a lot of tournaments when he was an amateur. He was the best. One day he decided to turn professional. All of a sudden he had obligations, challenges and lost all his spontaneity. He had lost his skill. I pointed out to him that when he was an amateur he didn't think about aiming at the hole. He simply decided to get the ball in and the rest just happened. Now, he was in a situation where he did it purposely, he thought about it, calculated and his conscious mind had taken over. So he decided to stop thinking and his skills returned. He had to re-learn what he knew at the outset, i.e. to let his unconscious mind gauge the exact distance between his feet and the hole. The only thing he consciously had to do was to enjoy himself.

A racing driver who drives at 190 mph will tell you that if he looks at an obstacle he will drive into it but if he looks elsewhere the car will follow the direction of his eyes. He doesn't think about what he has to do, it just happens.

Your mind simply needs precise details about what you want. It will then do the rest. Have you ever lost a friend in a crowd? How do you find him/her? After beginning by moaning, you scan the crowd but you must have that person's image in your mind. Then, lo and behold, you see him/her. This is because if you have a different image in your mind, e.g. your dog or your fridge, (i.e. if you think about something else, which brings to mind a different image) your mind wouldn't be able to detect the person.

An image is therefore essential and precision goes with it. Don't forget that for your mind everything is true; the real, the imaginary or the virtual. For your mind, a precise image conjured up in your thoughts is the same as a precise image of the person you are looking for in the crowd. Your mind will look for it and bring it to you. I hope you understand just how important this detail really is, as it determines the results in your life.

After the "visually **precise**", let us turn to the "auditory **precise**", (the words you say).

You know that to find the solution to a problem, what is said must be complete and precise.

If you want to meet the love of your life, find the ideal job or the perfect place to live, here is what you have to do. You will need a large sheet of paper, time to think and time to write it down.

If it concerns finding a job, don't pronounce the name of the profession. For example, if you want to become an artist don't say "singer, actor, writer or script writer" because your unconscious mind will have nothing more to do. Simply write down that you want to become an artist with everything that implies for you. Your mind will then do the rest by leading you to your true place.

For a place to live, don't say the name of a town or that you want to be close to the sea, as I have often heard. You will never find anything or nothing will happen. Simply tell your mind everything you desire. It will bring you exactly what you need and it will be even better than you had imagined.

What, in your view, are the ideal criteria? A criterion is a word, a small value: nice, calm, intelligent, distinguished, etc.

Question: *what do I expect from a man in life?*

Or *what do I expect from a woman in life?*

Or *what do I expect from a dwelling place in life?*

Or *what do I expect from a job?*

Let us take "looking for a man" as an example. If you don't have the example of a perfect couple in your genealogy, your unconscious mind cannot invent it and doesn't know what you want. This is why I asked you earlier to stop wasting time observing the mishaps of your elders and instead to set up a strategy to create new relationships and thereby a new life.

Write: what I expect from a man I share my life with:

CRITERIA (a word, a small value)	EQUIVALENTS (the concrete explanation of the word). What does this mean for me? How do I know he is…
Intelligent	He talks about everything and is interested in everything. I am proud of him.
Helpful	He helps me with everything (I strongly advise this).
Faithful	He is happy with me.
Tolerant	He accepts other people's points of view.
Handyman	He can do everything around the house (useful).
Clean	He washes himself (think of everything).

Think hard and long. To find a life partner, come up with at least **30 criteria** and write them down clearly and neatly. Take advantage of this exercise to decide what would be ideal for you. If the word exists, then the person exists. **You have the right to dream and to choose your life.** It will become precise. If you say: "I want to meet someone", your unconscious mind will indeed have you meet someone, anyone, on the basis of your family memories.

Decide what the person who will share your life "**will specifically be like**". I guess you are familiar with the expression: "You only have to ask…" it really is true.

If you have already been married or had a relationship, write down all the qualities you appreciated in this person and put an explanation opposite. Then note down all the things you didn't appreciate in him/ her and put the contrary of each word showing what you would like instead.

Don't forget to mention "long-lasting couple" if that's what you want. Stable and generous are also good. Funny too (he makes you laugh). This will always be better than a night dress.

For a job, try to remember a part time or short term job you've had and write down everything you liked about it. Then list everything you didn't like and write down their opposites, what you would like instead. Define about 15 criteria. Then note down all the values that the ideal job represents for you: satisfying, varied, fun, and don't forget "lucrative" (I can earn more than I need to pay the bills), with prospects, responsibilities or not, flexitime or not, compatible with family life or not, sedentary or not, etc.

For a place to live, here are a few example criteria:

Bright	The main rooms are bright. Facing south.
Spacious	Respects everyone's living space.
Prestige	Attractive, has style.
Pratical	I can walk to the market.

You can do this type of research for any objective you want.

Make two columns:

Criterion on the left (the word)	Its equivalent on the right (the explanation) "How specifically…".

When I separated from my third husband I decided to use this technique to find a suitable place to live for my sons and myself. I didn't use the word "house" or "apartment" as I didn't want to influence my mind. When I read out my criteria my mother said "that's going to be expensive". But I calmly thought about my ideal place to live: near woodland, spacious, bright with a big balcony and very peaceful. A place to live that suited my needs and my budget. I put this piece of paper on a shelf. A few weeks later I was at the bank with the lady who had been looking after my account for years. She was about to retire. She greeted me and asked me to sit down for a few minutes. I told her a little about my life and she said: "Oh dear, all these couples who are getting divorced! Look, here's the file of another young couple who are splitting up. Their apartment is up for sale and as they are in a hurry they have slashed the price. It' such a shame!"

"Really," I said, "could you tell me where their apartment is?"

She gave me the address. This was the only apartment I visited and I am still living there. It fitted all my criteria. It was perfect, comfortable and at a reasonable price. Everything went smoothly, like a dream.

Would I consciously have been able to do as well?

Again, as far as your mind is concerned, there is no such thing as easy or difficult.

Check now that your project is very **precise**. *You have stated the intention and the intention of this intention. You are able to conjure up a clear, precise image of it in colour. You have discovered in what way it is important for you, you have defined the values and criteria and you can now go on to the second parameter in two phases.*

Second parameter "Realistic and Responsible"

Above all, **realistic**.

Is it realistic to say that I can open a therapist consultancy after a 16 day training course? Obviously not. Nevertheless, how many people read one or two books on a subject and then set up business? It takes many years of study to become a doctor or a surgeon, a plumber or electrician, mechanic or painter (see chapter 7 on "The Laws Governing Success" by Herbert Armstrong). Everything is possible after a realistic time period during which learning and assimilation take place.

Is it realistic to buy a big BMW when you work on a factory production line with four children and a wife to feed on one small salary? It isn't but it may be if you change your job.

Dreaming is good and even necessary but it is just as important to take action. You have already discovered a series of ways to reach your goal. You now need to check it is realistic. If you don't really believe in it and your goal is unrealistic, you will never reach it.

- I need to believe in it.
- How, in concrete terms, am I going to do it?

Here again, when your unconscious mind knows what your intentions, criteria and values are, let yourself be guided and follow the ideas that come to you. Act on them and carry them out in the order they arrive. Your unconscious mind knows how to organise and divide them up into small tasks.

For those of you who are well familiar with the reflex answer: "Yes, but!" and who ignore their inner voice, try using the "Walt Disney technique" (Toolbox chapter). This will cure your little quirk forever.

As well as being realistic, it is essential to be **responsible for your project or objective**.

You are now familiar with meta programs and you know that people who fail are in an external frame of reference: "I was told that…" They wait for the opportunity, the opinion or the support of others or the last person to speak was right (I have given you several examples).

If a young man becomes an architect because his father asks him to take over the family business, he is in for a lot of problems. He will quite simply fail over a period of years or business will fall off sharply. When someone introduces you to a potential partner you should say: "No thanks, I'll make my own choice".

The choice and the approach depend entirely on you: "I'm the one who decides what is good or bad for me. I know what I have to do. I'm the one who wants. Everything I do is to that end. I am totally responsible".

No computer can solve the problem of another computer. Your unconscious mind has all the capabilities and potential to help you succeed by yourself. You have all the necessary resources inside you to make great changes or succeed in what you do but not what other people do.

Imagine a teacher who complains: "I've got problems in the classroom. The children should be quieter and more disciplined". This is indeed what happens in most cases. She doesn't feel responsible for making things better. She wants the children to change. Today we are seeing the result of this type of reasoning. If this teacher had the tools to motivate the children and make them listen to her, thinking: "I'm the one who's responsible for changing things in this classroom", all her problems would disappear.

How does one become interesting? When one is interested! (see the chapter "Toolbox": "Efficient Communication Technique - reformulation").

Teachers who take an interest in their students usually have interested students. Take an interest in what people are saying, give them importance and you will become interesting and important in their eyes.

When do people feel important? When we give them importance; (see the "feedback sandwich" in the chapter "Toolbox"). There are so many things that the school system needs to learn! A good way to start would be to change the negative and discouraging remarks on children's reports, e.g. a young boy called Julian had just proudly finished the final class of nursery school. He had received good points all year long and enjoyed going to school every day. He was about 5 years old. As he couldn't read he proudly gave his report to his father. On it was written: "Julien doesn't listen to other people".

His father, who up until then had admired everything Julian did and encouraged him as much as he could, then said: "ah, you see! How many times have I told you that you don't listen to what people say!" His elder brother was congratulated for his report but for the first time poor Julian understood that he'd lost the special relationship he had with his father and he developed a serious bout of scarlet fever. Well done teacher!! She could have made the same remarks using the sandwich technique as follows:

Julian has worked hard. He has deserved a lot of good points and should be proud of himself. It would be a good idea to work on improving his listening. But well done Julian you can be proud of yourself".

Here we are saying the same thing but with the motivation included. We should teach children to be proud of themselves. Indeed, Julian will unconsciously remember what he needs to improve.

For any objective, you should be entirely responsible for the choice, the decision, the solutions, the approach and your results.

This "being responsible" parameter exists for everything you experience in life. When you have a problem, don't make other people responsible for it because you then become a victim with no power to change anything. Make yourself totally responsible for what happens to you and you will find solutions.

The objective is therefore realistic...you are responsible for it.

We now come to the third parameter

Third parameter, "Ecological": Verification

"Ecology" means self respect, respect for the environment and for those around you. You can succeed perfectly well whilst at the same time preserving the interests of other people.

- I check this is in my best interests (I use the interests defined at the beginning).
- I totally agree with this. Every part of me agrees with it.

We are multi-faceted personalities. Part of me wants to go to bed early while another part wants to watch TV. Part of me wants to go on holiday whereas another part says: "you've got too much work". We are often like this. All our parts and our facets have a positive intention for us, a useful function. Each one of them defends very important values but not the same ones. Sometimes these different parts get in each other's way, at other times they are totally opposed and prevent each other from functioning.

- A young woman thought she had a psychological problem because she couldn't choose between two jackets, one size 40 and the other size 42. So she didn't buy either. She understood that the intention of the part of her that wanted size 40 was to be feminine as it showed off her figure. The part of her that preferred size 42 wanted to be comfortable and at ease. After doing a quick mental technique with her, she decided to buy a jacket that was both feminine and comfortable. She respected the values of both her parts and in this way was in total agreement about buying that jacket.

Let's take a young woman who wants to be a nurse. Part of her is very tempted and has already made up her mind but another part of her thinks about the fact that she doesn't like injections. She can also say to herself: "yes it's good to be a nurse but it's not very well paid" or "I'm going to choose to be a nurse but the hours of work aren't easy" and so on. She will never be happy in her job. Part of her wants to do it but another part of her is afraid, in opposition or doesn't have the same opinion.

For any personal objective you have, check that all the different parts of you are in agreement. When an objective is collective and involves the responsibility of others, all those concerned need to be in agreement.

Imagine a woman who tells her husband: "darling, I've invited the Smiths for dinner on Saturday". "You could have asked me first," he retorts, angrily. She immediately thinks that he is bad-tempered but she's not been at all "ecological".

When we have an objective that involves others, it is essential for each party to agree and be responsible.

She could have said: "I'd thought of inviting the Smiths on Saturday evening. What do you think?" In this way he would very probably have agreed and have been much more pleasant.

Question: *do I entirely agree with that? Do all the parts of me really agree?*

- When putting your plan into action, you need to check there are **no disadvantages** for others or for the **environment** and that your objective is in the best interests of everyone.

  You will find this parameter in the chapter on "Abundance". When your actions do not take the well-being of others into consideration, over a period of months or years, nothing will work.

Question: *will there be any disadvantages for one or more people in my circle of friends or family? Who is concerned by my plan?*

CREATE THE LIFE YOU WANT

In order to be ecological we can, depending on the context: warn, announce, prepare, propose, ask or act with respect for others whilst preserving each person's interests.

Ecology also means respecting past experience, things that are passive and preserving what has been learned (the secondary benefits).

Let's take the first day of a new Managing Director in a big company. He calls a staff meeting and introduces himself: "Good morning to you all, I am your new managing director and this is what I plan to do together…". He gives an excellent speech but by the end many of them are feeling hostile towards him. What went wrong?

He didn't say: "I've studied what you've done and achieved and I'm impressed. You've come a long way. I want to keep all the major changes you have introduced. Now, I would like to give you my suggestions". If he respects the past and keeps what has been learned, there is a good chance that everyone will be on his side and he will get off to a good start.

Divorce also means respecting ecology. First of all, give the couple a chance. Fifteen or twenty years of married life plus children together certainly deserves a family reframing and a pause for thought. As I explained above, the couple can define what they expect from a man or a woman. They then exchange what they have written to see whether or not they are capable of this. They then need to determine a common vision of the ideal couple.

After many years of married life, couples very often discover that they both had a very different vision of what a couple should be. All this should of course be studied BEFORE getting married. In this way, many divorces would be avoided.

After this exchange, if love has really disappeared, the parents can get the children together and explain the situation (in a sandwich— see "Toolbox"). The good points of Mum or Dad should be highlighted and then they can separate by mutual consent, with peace of mind.

For example, the father might say: "your mother and I got married for love and we have had many delightful years together. She is a wonderful woman and a very good mother. But we have come to the point where we are no longer on the same wavelength. We argue a lot and life together has become difficult. It would be much better if we could both meet someone we get on better with. But you're not going to lose your father or your mother, who will always remain my best friend".

A child doesn't suffer from a divorce. What hurts a child are the constant arguments and hearing one of the parents criticise or belittle the other. The father should remain a hero and the mother a wonderful woman. Try at least not to argue in front of the children so they don't suffer.

When ecology is respected, children remain well-balanced and their school work doesn't suffer.

We could write a whole book on the parameter of ecology. Even when parking our car, thinking about others is ecological.

Who teaches teenagers that after 10 p.m. we should speak more softly, that we must respect those who have to get up to go to work early the next morning or those who are ill? In the summer holidays you can hear young people at a loose end in front of their apartment blocks shouting, laughing and screaming until the early hours of the morning and their parents do nothing about it. Every parent is responsible for teaching this. But children don't do what you say, they do what you do. Which adults give a good example?

We would like children to remain seated in class and to arrive on time. I have noticed in seminars that very few adults are able to do this. Are we capable of doing what we ask our children to do?

This is what is taught for roughly 15 years: "before the age of 18 you don't have the right to do what you can do later". As the French singer Daniel Balavoine sang, young people want "later" to be "right now". They don't want to wait until they are old to do what they want. As their parents don't respect the environment, neither do they.

When it comes to determining an objective, the simple fact of "not respecting" ecology can lead to short term or long term failure. As we are multi-faceted beings, all the parts of your personality must be in agreement without there being any disadvantage for others.

We can now go on to the last point:

Fourth paramèter: Measurable

- What realistic time deadline do I fix for myself to reach my objective? Without this deadline you might reach your objective in your next life. Indeed, if the deadline is not realistic you will say "I failed". In fact, you won't have failed. It was simply that your deadline was not realistic.
- How will I know? How will I know this objective is the right one? How will I know whether I made the right choice?

It is by asking yourself these questions that you will be sure your objective is the right one, that you are going in the right direction and that you can reach it.

You will find the summary telling you how to determine an objective in the chapter "Toolbox" and you can practise by following the different steps of the technique.

- See the advantages.
- Check the fears and find solutions.

Present state – Desired state

- PRÉCISE
- RÉALISTIC, RESPONSIBLE
- ECOLOGICAL
- MEASURABLE

Select an experience that went wrong and check for 1 or more missing parameters.

This is one of the keys to success.

Now, practise this for small things to check that the magic is in you.

For years I used to go to work by car. My consultancy was on the Champs-Elysées in Paris and I used to park in rue Washington. Anyone who knows the area will tell you that it's almost impossible to find a parking space in this very busy street. An underground car park that I have never used is available for visitors. For over 10 years I always used to park in more or less the same place in front of a Chinese restaurant. When I left home I would say to myself: "it's precise, I'll park in rue Washington". I could see the exact spot with my internal movie camera, I told my mind what time I would arrive (not always the same) and I created an emotion. It was realistic. If other cars managed to park in this street why couldn't I? It was responsible,

I wanted it and it was in my best interests. It was perfectly ecological as I was in total agreement and I parked as well as possible so as not to bother others. It was measurable, 10 or 11 a.m. PREM! I thanked my unconscious mind in advance for reserving my place (be polite with your unconscious mind).

I then put on the radio and thought about other things as I was totally sure I would find a parking space. When I arrived at the Champs-Elysées roundabout I said aloud: "I'll be arriving in about 5 minutes, thank you". I arrived in rue Washington and lo and behold either the space was free or someone was about to leave. This happened every week for over 10 years. It wasn't luck or chance but programming (chance does not exist).

Recently, one of my students was looking for a new place to live with his girlfriend in Paris and was getting worried because he hadn't found anything. He had given a month's notice on the very dark apartment he was in and was due to move by the end of November. By mid October he was extremely anxious and despite everything I had taught him he was starting to get on my nerves. I asked them both to write down all the criteria they required for the perfect place to live (criteria – equivalents).

They put "bright, classy, in a wealthy neighbourhood, matches our needs and budget and so on." Obviously, at first sight it may have seemed out of their budget range. Nevertheless, it was **P**recise, **R**ealistic for them (young dreamers), **R**esponsible (it was their decision), **E**cological (they both agreed on it and there were no disadvantages for the environment), **M**easurable (their deadline was the end of November).

On the 28th of October he got a 'phone call from the estate agent saying there was a free apartment in the very attractive 16th arrondissement of Paris. They made the acquaintance of an elderly man who explained that rather than increasing the rent, he preferred to have a reliable couple who could give him guarantees. The apartment is superb. All the criteria have been satisfied as if by magic and the rent is exactly the same as they were paying in the flat they had left.

The PREM was perfect. My student and his girlfriend didn't set mental limits by imagining that their criteria would be impossible. They simply entrusted their unconscious mind with their wishes and it did the rest. Of course, they had remembered to give arguments "when…as soon as…the day after the day I…"

It's like a game. Everything is possible for your "computer" as soon as it has understood your intentions and has the exact description of the problem.

William James, the oldest of American psychologists, said in his book "The Gospel of Relaxation": "once the decision has been taken let it act and don't worry about the outcome. Release your intellectual and practical mechanism, let it act at will, this way it will do you twice as many favours. The path to success goes via peace of mind, abdication, not via tension but by relaxation."

To efficiently create the life you want, there is one more small but essential detail. How can we be sure of our own power over ourselves? By changing our limiting or disempowering beliefs. These have a great effect on the outcomes in our life.

Also, by having the capacity to solve any problem using our own thought.

For this, we will now discover the logical levels.

Chapter V

The Logical Levels of Thought
or How to Solve a Problem

The anthropologist Gregory Bateson originated a model of logical levels in 1973 and Robert Dilts gave us some applications for them in 1989. I introduced some new applications myself in 1998 for conflict solving. This knowledge could be used in the same way as we use a calculator, to solve all personal, family and professional problems.

Our thought is organised into a hierarchy at different levels, called "logical levels".

Each level solves and organises the information for the level below it

The role of thought is not to find solutions but to think correctly. When a problem arises at one level of thought we can go higher up to solve things lower down. Changing something at the upper levels will always make a difference at the lower levels at the same time. Read this sentence several times to understand the process.

Einstein said: "we can not solve a problem at the same level it was created".

Where does our lack of capabilities come from?

Does it come from our beliefs?

Does it come from the vision we have of ourselves or from the role that we play in a life that isn't right for us?

How can we get rid of fear, stress, anxiety and all such disempowering emotions? By becoming aware of our levels of thought and by going as high as possible in our reasoning. We can bring about change by understanding and identifying the levels and the way in which they affect us.

Look at this diagram starting at the bottom.

> The role of one level is to solve and organise the one below it.

TRANSMISSION

MISSION
The role I play in life, what I do to satisfy my vision, my dream, in accordance with my values.

VISION
What would the ideal be?

IDENTITY
Who am I? – How do I recognise myself?
What does this prove about me?

BELIEFS	VALUES
What I believe or believed.	What I am looking for. E.g: love, recognition, respect, etc.

EMOTIONS – FEELINGS
What do I feel?
What did I feel?

CAPABILITIES
What capabilities do I need?
When I am told it is difficult, I can not do it.

BEHAVIOUR
(Illness is a behaviour)
What do I do? – How do I behave?
What behaviour have I set up?

ENVIRONMENT
Everything around me: my family, people, my job, the coercive elements around me.

The environment

This means people, your family, your job, means of transport, where you live and all the coercive elements of the environment.

When something doesn't suit you in your environment, it is no use waiting for things to change. If you died on the spot nothing would change. If your mother in law is nasty, your son disobedient or your husband disrespectful towards you, there is no point making yourself ill, getting annoyed or getting depressed, this will not change anything. However, you may be able to go up to the level above: the behaviour level.

Behaviour

IIf you alter your **behaviour** towards your mother in law (as well as your own interpretations) and learn to communicate with your son, things may become different. Illness is a behaviour. As you haven't found a solution higher up in the logical levels, illness sets in and organises the environment (your children are nicer, your husband looks after you, you receive a disability allowance and so on).

Any behaviour you set up has a useful or positive function. It is much better to find out what the useful function of a behaviour is than to clash with it or try to change it at all costs.

This level provides an answer to the question: "What have you done? or "What have I done?" "I left, I slammed the door, I hung up etc".

Obviously, the behaviour itself is the consequence of a higher logical level, e.g. of a belief. We can check on this. Your behaviour influences the environment. Some people know how to make very good use of this.

Setting up new behaviours that are appropriate to each situation will help you change or create your environment (see the chapter "Toolbox"). You now know that your mind believes in the behaviour you have enacted.

An idea, a thought → gives you a physiology (the face, the expression that matches what you are thinking) → which gives you your behaviour → your brain immediately makes an evaluation, an estimation → which brings a conclusion → which gives you a belief.

But the belief is not a fact. You create the fact. What can we do to change the belief or the thought? We can obviously act upon the thought, upon the idea itself and this would change it immediately, (don't change a thought by willpower. Replace it by another thought). We can also act on behaviour and this will lead the mind to other estimations, other conclusions and therefore to other beliefs.

When we listen to someone talking, it's easy to recognise the level at which he/she is thinking. You might hear: "I smoke because it helps me fit more easily into the groups around the coffee machine". This person smokes at the **environment** level and the patch system should be able to help him/her stop. Someone else says: "I smoke because it helps my composure. I don't know what to do with my hands." This person smokes at the level of **behaviour**. Someone else may say: "I smoke because it helps me think better, it gives me ideas." This person smokes at the level of **capabilities**. The patch will not be effective at all levels.

Capabilities

Saying or thinking: "It's difficult, it's not easy, it's very hard and I'll never manage!" means you have a problem at the logical level of **capabilities**.

"What capabilities do I need to live in this environment with the behaviour I have set up?"

As the role of each logical level is to organise the information for level below it, it is not by making a room more comfortable that your capabilities will suddenly appear or multiply.

- When my children were not doing well at school I gave them a nice office to work in with shelf room. In this case, I worked on the lower level in order to improve the upper level and I can now say that what I did was of no use whatsoever. Where does this lack of capability come from? Let us go higher up.

Emotions, feelings. Internal states

Stress, anxiety, fear, panic or annoyance influence all the levels below. Your capabilities are blocked. You set up inadequate or despicable behaviour and in the environment the outcome is horrible. In fact you attract people and situations that make you experience exactly what you don't want.

Any therapy that aims to treat emotions at the level of emotions will prove totally useless and you can follow one for 15 years without getting any significant results. As long as you believe what you believe, you will continue to feel the same emotions.

Where do these emotions and feelings come from? Let's go higher up in the logical levels.

All the higher levels will provide you with solutions to cure anxiety, stress or fear.

Beliefs and values

When a student thinks he is useless, that school is difficult and too demanding, the outcome is: he is anxious, he cancels out his capabilities, behaves like a dunce and finds people in the environment to prove he is right.

A belief is a generalisation of an event or a fact that you believe to be true. It is a powerful emotional state of certainty that you have about people, things and events.

You have created this certainty using your own terms, i.e. images created in your head that are increasingly clear, distinct, in colour and close to you. These are often interpretations, false perceptions and pre-suppositions. A belief has the power to kill or cure. If you have limiting, disempowering beliefs about yourself, the world and everything around you, your whole life is influenced by this.

People (the environment) behave towards you on the basis of your beliefs and the expectations of your mind. All the subjective representations you have created in your mind have become reality.

Our beliefs have an impact on the outcome of everything we do. We influence our objectives by the basic premises we hold about them and about how to reach them. Beliefs have a "creative prediction" value (self fulfilling and self creating prophecies).

Absolute certainty lies at this level of beliefs. So, choose beliefs that are favourable to change, to communication and to learning, beliefs that are result-oriented. Then take them on board **as if** they were true.

When a child is anxious or stressed out at school, helping her stay calm won't improve her capabilities or change her attitude to studying. We need to find out what she thinks about herself, about school, about the teachers and so on.

One day a woman of 51 told me:

—"I'm afraid of rules, of being dependent and that stresses me out."

—"OK! Give me a rule that stresses you out."

—"Being on time."

Imagine a primary school teacher who begins her class at 9 a.m. A pupil arrives at 9.15. If the teacher is thorough she will go over everything she has just said or done so the child won't be lost but this is impossible for the rest of the class. Now, if the teacher just carries on the child will have missed the beginning and there is some information he won't have. Imagine a train that doesn't leave at 7.12 but when there is no-one left on the platform. Many people will be late for work.

This woman has confused "rule" with organisation, planning, ecology (no drawbacks for others). Her fear of rules is the consequence of a belief or, as we will see later on, an incorrect or unpleasant vision of her parents, educators or both.

The problem isn't within the problem but in the perception that we have of things, of people or of events. It is this woman's perception that has created the problem and wanting to solve it or change things has given rise to stress.

Wanting nothing, taking things as they come, expecting the best in an inquisitive manner and adapting to circumstances. This is the beginning of happiness.

Regarding her fear of dependence I asked: "what does that mean for you, being afraid of dependence?"

"Being obliged to follow or to do something I don't want to do or that doesn't correspond to who I am," she replied. "OK, give me an example."

"My father forced me to learn the piano."

What would have happened if the child had understood the positive intention of her father? Maybe he wanted to help his daughter as he was a musician himself or maybe he wanted to give her knowledge that would last her a lifetime? What would have happened if the little girl had thought: "later on, I'll choose a different instrument. I'll play the guitar or I'll stop music altogether then I'll be free". Her perception has again caused a problem. This child could have chosen to be flexible, to accept, to be curious and take pleasure in creating her future. She could also have chosen to express herself or even to consider what she would get out of it. We are all confronted with a multitude of choices. Now she had become an adult this woman thought she had to obey and accept other people's wishes.

Many people think that when their relatives say something, they ought to agree with them... Not at all. Or they would like others to agree with them... Wrong too. Everyone has the right to express their ideas and you have a perfect right not to agree with them.

Look for the positive intention, the useful function or sometimes the mitigating circumstances and limitations. **People do not want to be right, they want to be understood.**

Let's take a woman who complains that she feels sad, frustrated and misunderstood when her family criticises her around the table (criticism is a perception in itself). I asked her the sort of criticism she gets: "For example when I make a cake. I put a lot of love into making it but my children say it's not nice. I feel worthless and unimportant".

What a belief! The children are not saying that their mother is useless. Neither do they doubt that a lot of love went into making the cake. They are simply giving their opinion. What would happen if she were to ask them: What's wrong with the recipe?" Maybe the cake is too dry, too sweet or too soft. Maybe the recipe really isn't good. In any case it's not tasty as far as the children are concerned. This woman would really like her children to enjoy the cake or wants them to pretend to enjoy it.

Let's imagine that she looks for the "useful function" in her children's remarks. The children have taste and they refuse to eat something just because they have been given it. They are in an internal frame of reference and this is excellent. Moreover, this says nothing at all about the mother. If this woman changes the rule she has placed under her values "gratitude and appraisal", if she accepts that her children are entitled to an opinion that is different from hers, she can then ask them what type of cake they would like. This won't take away the fact that she still puts a lot of love into making it and that she is a good mother.

There is no difference between a belief and a value. In a value, we find a system of beliefs and one or more values in a belief. This is why beliefs and values are situated at the same logical level.

All your emotions are merely the outcome of limiting and disempowering beliefs (change in belief) or of an infringed value (that we believe has been infringed) that has not been satisfied in everyday life. Your feelings may also come from a lack of identity or, higher up, from an nasty view of life, of oneself or of others. At the very top of the logical levels, stress may also be the result of a role (a mission) you are playing in life that doesn't suit you at all.

You can "hunt down" your beliefs and enter into hand to hand combat with them (to change them, see the belief techniques in the chapter: "Toolbox").

When you believe something negative about yourself or about other people, ask yourself the question: "what could be the use of the images I'm creating? What is the use of what I believe? And what if this belief was wrong?"

Values

One of the reasons children have negative beliefs about school, lessons and homework is that they put no value into what they do and don't see the importance of being good learners. Still further, if they have values such as recognition or appraisal, they think that the environment (parents or teachers) should give them some. This means they have one or several beliefs that prevent them blossoming (these are rules that the children have put under their values).

Values tell us what is important for us, what we are looking for, e.g. love, freedom, creativity, self-fulfilment, success, health, friendship etc.

Values are often the cause of many misunderstandings, arguments, wars, prejudices, conflicts or lack of communication.

Values in all fields are at the very heart of change and have a decisive impact on our life. This is because our emotions (feelings), our capabilities and behaviours depend on whether or not our values are satisfied in our life and on the meaning of the belief we put under them.

When we stake claim to a value (justice – respect – security), we think this is normal, universal and that everyone should have this value. But there are over 70 of them and you can not possess them all. When you expect "respect" in a particular situation, another person will perhaps act on "curiosity, friendship, conviviality or pleasure".

Someone who likes cleanliness and tidiness, for example, will of course, think that this value is important and obvious, that everyone should take off their shoes and do the vacuum cleaning. But this person's children live according to different values such as "adventure, freedom, joy" and will develop cleanliness later in life.

When a value is important for you, it belongs to you and the logical levels demonstrate that the environment can not satisfy them in your place because the role of one level is to organise the information for the level below. However, you can learn a communication technique that will show people around you the advantages of sharing your value.

We should all satisfy our values in our daily lives without expecting anything from other people. Children often say to me:

—*My father doesn't tell me it's good.*

—*My mother doesn't kiss me.*

—*I don't get any compliments, I feel worthless and unaccepted.*

Teach your children the following:

How to discover the belief, the rule we have placed under a value?

Ask yourself the following question: "what needs to happen for me to be recognised? What is needed for me to feel worthy or loved?

Your answer is your rule (your belief)

All values are excellent and interesting. It is the rules and beliefs you have placed under them that disturb you and which can very often cost you dearly.

There are two ways to be unhappy in life:

The first way: when your rules are too rigid. For example, I need to get 18 or 19/20 to be considered a good student. This is an excellent way to get stressed out because it's too rigid. You'd do better to loosen up this rule and accept lower grades, sometimes even a bad grade. It is only a result and you will be able to improve by studying this result. Be flexible with yourself.

Another example: "To be a good mother, my home should always be clean and tidy. Dinner should be served at 7 p.m., the children in bed by 8.30 p.m. and not a speck of dust on the furniture". This is another good way to spoil your life and that of others. Life will be much more pleasant if you loosen up this rule and emphasise "Love, Joy, Laughter, Humour and Flexibility".

Many women have imposed rules on themselves that they are now incapable of breaking, thereby thrusting their limitations and unhappiness upon others.

Look at this rule: "I can't go to gym in the evening because I have the meal to prepare and it has to be ready when my husband comes home". "What would happen if dinner wasn't ready when your husband came home?" "Nothing".

So, she can go to gym.

Your husband hasn't asked you to make the house spotless or to be there when he comes home. This is often a rule you have imposed on yourself and you complain to others that you have too much to do. I've often heard the phrase: "with everything I do for you". Well... in that case do a little less and look after your smile, your femininity and exuberance instead because your husband most certainly prefers something more than a clean house to come home to. And very often nobody has asked you to do it anyway.

Do things because you enjoy them or because you want to. This is no longer a rule but a game or a pleasure. Now, if your husband really wants you to be there with the meal ready when he gets home and this is a drag for you, get him to review his own rules and organise a reframing of the couple.

Loosen up your rules. Even better, get rid of them! In the chapter: "Toolbox", look at the four behaviours we set up described by transactional analysis. This will help you understand what makes you act in this way.

One day, as I had taken on a lot of work to provide for my family, I organised a "debate over dinner" at home. I used to organise dinners with a discussion topic that I called "debate over dinner". With the children we would talk about subjects that interested everyone so as to improve family life. That evening in the presence of my husband, my eldest son (17) and second son (15) I announced the topic which in fact was a decision I had taken: "I've decided that I'm not going to cook the evening meal any more unless I really want to". There was a long silence around the table. You could hear a pin drop. But we were soon in the process of discussing how things would be organised.

I drew up a plan in the kitchen:

- One protein (meat – fish – egg – cheese – tofu). One of you can look after that, it's easy. Get out a slice of ham and the cheese. They learned to prepare fish and I taught them a few things.
- Vital food (green vegetables and salads). Someone else can look after that. I taught them to fry vegetables and prepare a mixed salad.
- A starch (pasta – rice – potatoes – lentils). Someone else for this.
- Dessert—ready to eat in the fridge. You just have to get it out. Some families give this responsibility to the youngest child.

   I discovered that the expression "no-one is irreplaceable" is indeed true. In the end, we all had a lot of fun. If this hadn't been the case I would have asked them all to review their own rules.

   Some time later, and again around the table, I told them I was going to stop doing the ironing. We all went through a long learning process and, as I refused to give in, my sons are now experts at ironing (which has been a great help and source of relief for their respective wives).

The second way to be unhappy in life is when your rules deprive you of power. You have no power when you are unable to control your rules and you can not control them when they depend on other people.

What would need to happen for you to feel loved in your life? If you answer; "my husband would have to give me flowers, come home earlier in the evening, surprise me etc. or my children should be more affectionate". This is a very good way to be unhappy.

If your husband doesn't conform to your rule, you get depressed.

In fact, you are unhappy when people infringe your belief, when they don't act as you would like them to, when things don't work out the way you had planned or wanted. In short, when people or events do not conform to your rules. Your values are not satisfied when they depend on others.

You will always be happy if you take things as they come, without expecting anything and without comparing them with other experiences. Indeed, if all the values that are important for you depend entirely on you, with no rules, you will succeed in life and you will very rarely fall ill.

Nothing and no-one can change the way you feel, except yourself. You can give yourself more power by modifying your rules, e.g. I am happy every time I express love. Love depends on you, it is your value. It belongs to you and it is up to you to satisfy it in everyday life.

Get rid of your rules!!

Let's imagine that the belief placed under the value "respect" is that other people should respect you. You will be living in a permanent disillusion. Now, if you respect yourself and others, what they do and what they think, if you respect the environment and the rules of society which are not strict rules but rules enabling us to live together, then you will be respected.

Parents must respect their children for their children to respect them. This means listening to them (children often call their mother a dozen times before she answers), taking an interest in what they say, in their ideas and their fears. Parents must also respect the environment (not argue in front of others, smoke outside, be quiet after 10 p.m. etc.)

I remember seeing a young man without a ticket jump over the barriers in the Gare de Lyon train station in Paris. The police stopped him and asked him for his identity papers. I heard the young man say: "you owe me some respect!" Strange thing to say wasn't it?

Imagine someone says to you: "you're really dumb!"

What would happen if you acted on the principle that this person has the right to believe this, that you respect her point of view and then set about discovering how to appear less "dumb" in her eyes? This person hasn't been disrespectful to you. She has a different opinion from you, that's all. It is up to you to make her change her mind if you want to. It is also reassuring to know that when people speak, they are only speaking about themselves. This says nothing about you.

For example, a father says to his son: "You're really useless!" The boy would really have understood what was going on if he had answered: "No dad it's not because you can't manage to make me understand things that you're useless. You do the best you can, that's all."

A woman who remarried complained that the sons of her new husband didn't respect her. For several years the boys had lived with their parents and suddenly they found themselves being ordered around by another woman. I asked her: "Have you asked them about their habits, what they like to eat, how their mother said goodnight to them and so on". "No, not at all" she replied. This woman was imposing new rules and a new life without respecting the old one. It was up to her to apply her value "respect" so that the children would follow her. (I give this example in the chapter: "Toolbox").

Let's take the value "beauty and aesthetics". This is important for many of us. Some women don't like themselves. They think they are overweight, unattractive and are very jealous and possessive. They project their malaise onto their husband and as they don't love themselves they believe their husband doesn't love them either. The result of this is that they want to shoot down anything feminine that moves in the vicinity of their husband. This is unbearable.

Learn to love yourself and you can change everything. There are many ways you can improve your waistline, your face, your hair and become more attractive…and more seductive! (for your husband only, of course).

I explained all this to the 57 year old wife of a lawyer. She told me she'd worked for him since she was 23. Since he'd opened his business she had organised all the secretarial side. She told me: "I don't get any recognition. My husband doesn't realise that without me he couldn't work the way he does. He never says anything nice and I'm not paid a salary, everything goes into a common account".

So I set about explaining to this woman that the world is a mirror. A human being is like a bottle. Inside the bottle are nuclear particles and there are also nuclear particles outside the bottle. Therefore it is the same thing and everything moves around in lemniscate, i.e. in a large ∞. Everything you create inside yourself has repercussions on the outside. I explained that it was not up to her husband to give her recognition or self esteem but that it was up to her to do this.

This woman was very intelligent. She immediately put into practise what she had learned. When her husband was away on business she reorganised her office. She had some new white curtains put up, put a superb bouquet of imitation flowers in a large vase, bought herself two smart "designer" suits, had her hair cut and blond streaks put in. I hadn't seen the office before these changes but I saw it when they invited me over to tell me their story. On the door she had put up a sign saying "director's assistant, do not disturb". When her husband returned home in the evening he made no comment on her streaks or hairdo. The next morning she went off to work before him and closed her office door. When he arrived he obviously saw the sign "director's assistant, do not disturb". He knocked on the door and heard "Come in". He walked in and looked in surprise at the transformation; how elegant his wife looked, her new hairdo, the flowers, the perfume…a whole new world. He didn't say anything but went into the corridor to get a chair. He came back and sat down in front of his wife's desk and looking her straight in the eyes said: "how about discussing your salary?" Her eyes filled up with tears. That day she understood that the world was indeed a mirror and that she was the one who should first recognise her own value.

Buy yourself flowers every week, treat yourself to little gifts from time to time and if you think you have done something well, get your family together and tell them: "I'm very pleased with myself, I really like what I've done". You will start to feel happier. Of course, you've all heard the expression: "You're big headed!" "Not at all, I just have a good opinion of myself".

On the evening of a concert, a very disturbed looking young man arrived. He had a stomach ache and sweaty hands because he was due to play piano. In his head he had the criteria "skill, perfection, performance" but these criteria were all his own. He wasn't aware that those of the spectators were very different and much more accessible: "curiosity, conviviality, pleasure of the moment, enjoyment". Simply accepting to change his over-ambitious values would lessen his stress and anxiety. Things will be perfect if this young man adds simplicity and humour.

CREATE THE LIFE YOU WANT

He may also discover that he attaches far too much importance to others. He creates an internal image of himself: small whereas the others are very tall. If he changes his image and sees the others as being small with a big red nose, Mickey mouse ears and naked, his fear wil disappear.

All the values that are very important for you depend only on you. You will be in control of your destiny when the only source of your emotions is yourself.

Here are three ways to work on values and radically change your life. It's child's play.

An example for the value "money".

VALUE	What is my intention?	What am I going to do in real terms, on a daily basis, to satisfy this value in a win/win context? (good for me, good for others).
⇩	⇩	⇩
MONEY	Able to pay for what I need without thinking about it and living well.	Let's start with other people: what I do is useful. I am improving a system. I answer people's needs, I help and provide services. I use my skills and improve them. In my view: I am in the right place, I like what I do, I love it and I put a lot into it.

There are three parameters which will satisfy your value on a daily basis:

1. What I do in real terms for myself: an action, a result.
2. How I communicate this value to those around me in an ecological way.
3. I apply it for others and accept that others do the same.

To finish with the value: "money". I accept that other people earn money, my taxes are useful, (if you think this way, there is a good chance you are rich).

Let us take the value "Freedom":

VALUE ⇩	What is my intention? ⇩	What am I going to do in real terms on a daily basis to satisfy this value in a win/win context? (good for me good for others). ⇩
FREEDOM	Do what I want. Windsurfing or hiking.	I sign up for activities. I take part in these activities in a way that is ecological for my family and I get my message across elegantly. I accept the same thing for my children and spouse. They are free, I accept their ideas and I teach them to act without bothering others.

Teach your children to be pleased with themselves, to be proud of what they have done without waiting for their parents or teachers to compliment them. Because later in life if they expect their employer to praise what they have done they may well be disappointed or frustrated. They get paid, that's enough. They'll work in a win/win context so as to continually improve their conditions and those of others, proud of what they are doing. If they want a hug, they should go and ask for one. For those who think: "my mother never used to kiss and hug me", did they have a "I want a kiss and hug" sign stuck on their forehead?

If affection is your value, who is stopping you giving or asking for some?

The value "safety" can't be satisfied by the environment. Of course, it is 50/50. It is a good thing to drive more slowly. Four and a half million years ago when man came out of his cave, he looked to the right and to the left to check that a bear wasn't heading his way and then went off to fish in the lake. Four and a half million years later we've forgotten how to do this. Not only do we not teach our children how to cross a street, we now stop the cars so they can cross safely. The result is that we now see people walking anywhere and even darting in front of cars because they have learned that cars should stop to let them pass. A car will always arrive too fast for a pedestrian who is walking in the middle of the road in a bend or who crosses the road on a red light.

At school we could teach children to stay back in a safety zone during a car or bicycle race, thereby creating their own safety. A teenage girl dressed in a mini-skirt and a plunging low cut top, needs to be taught not to let a stranger walk her home at night.

We must be aware that there is danger on the streets, predators and that the role we have to play is that of creating our own safety. In this way, people would also start to believe that our behaviour can make others feel safe. But individuals cannot have this awareness because everyone expects safety to be provided by the government or other people.

Many children expect everything from others. In my seminars on "Success at School", I ask them "Who's got some pocket money?" "Me !" comes he answer, as almost everyone puts their hand up. "Shame on you!" I reply. They all put their arm down. Money is a value like any other. It all depends on the way this value is developed and the explanation given to it. From an early age children are taught that it is natural for parents to give them pocket money. Everything is upside down!

"How much do you think is the ideal amount? 15 $ (10 £) or 30 $ (20 £) per week? What do you do to deserve that? What role do you play?"

Let's go higher up in the logical levels (look in the chapter: "Toolbox" for the "Values technique and changing the rules." This will radically change your life).

Immediately alter the rules that you have set up under your values whilst asking yourself this first question:

- What is most important for me today? What gives meaning to my life? (Love – harmony – peace – self fulfilment – freedom – courage, etc.).

Make a list of at least 50 or 60 values. Choose 7 of them and ask yourself the following question for each one of them:

- What do I need for this value to be satisfied and what do I do in real terms on a daily basis, to develop and live it out?

If you do nothing, decide now what you're going to do, that would depend only on you.

In addition, when you initiate an action, check that the value placed under it is simple and easy to satisfy.

For example: "What does speaking in public imply?" Someone who is good at it will answer: "Enjoyment, humour, above all simplicity and having a welcoming attitude". Someone who is not good at it will answer: "Skill and being very precise". Such values deprive people of their power as they are too high or too rigid.

The essential question will be: "what does doing this or that imply in terms of values,?" Answer in very simple values.

Identity

Who are we if our values are given to us by the environment? We are nothing, no-one.

As soon as you say "I am" you are speaking at the logical level of identity.

What a pity that the identity of a woman should depend on the social status of her husband or that the identity of a young man depends on how much money his father has.

When children have worked hard at school to make a future for themselves, it's good to help them if you can. Because they have taken the trouble to obtain the standard of living they wanted. They have created their own identity.

But if some of them have spent their time going out, having fun, sleeping in late, womanising and refusing to have their own vision of life—the lazy devils—they don't deserve help. Let them live the way they have chosen or not chosen, even if it is hard for you. The French writer La Fontaine depicted this wonderfully in "The cicada and the ant". If they react and eventually create their own identity, then you can help them out. For that, they will need to go higher up in the logical levels.

To acquire a strong identity, answer the following questions: "How do I recognise myself?" Who am I? What type of person am I?" First of all, you need to have dreams, a beautiful vision of the world and to change the way you look at life and things, i.e. go up to the level above.

In the vision

The vision answers the question: what would the ideal be? For children who want pocket money it could be: "how much do you need?"

By definition, a vision is utopian. It is a dream lying dormant inside us that continues to motivate the child within us. Nothing exists–planes, trains, cars, glasses—that hasn't been dreamed up in someone's mind at some point. The greatest feats and achievements all started out in someone's dream.

If not only you don't dream and the only vision you have is focused on your misfortunes and everything you regret, then of course all the lower logical levels will be boiling over. The more beautiful your vision, the more your life will resemble it and the same goes for a negative vision.

You can have a vision on any subject: a company, a couple, education etc. In a couple, it is best for both partners to have the same vision. The same for a company; if the employees don't have the same vision as the boss there will obviously be problems.

You can change your vision of the people around you. Look for their positive intention.

Children have a vision of the world that is different from that of their parents. Let them dream. They have utopian dreams and they need them. Don't spoil them, go inside with them. One day they will accomplish great things. Intelligence means developing our creativity.

The vision answers the question: "what would be ideal for me in such and such a field?"

For people who don't know what to do with their lives, what role to play, mission to fulfil or what job to do, one single technique will provide the solution; the logical levels. For young students who are having doubts about their choices or for retired people who want to be useful after retiring, the following question will be the key.

How do we find our way?

Take a pen and paper and answer this: "if I had a magic wand and could create a perfect and wonderful world, what type of world would I create? What, in my opinion, is a wonderful world?" Again, your answer will be utopian. It is a dream, you must want it.

A young man who was getting nowhere at school gave me this answer: "for me, a perfect world would be one where everyone respects the eco-system and fish wouldn't have to eat any artificial fish food". His father got worried when he heard this and said: "you see, he's hopeless".

A man in his fifties was an architect. He had taken over his father's business but it wasn't really what he wanted to do (external frame of reference). As the years slipped by, business dropped off, he started drinking, his wife left him and he clung to his car, the last remnant of his glory. He had run out of money and felt lost.

He answered the question by saying: "for me, a wonderful world is a world where everyone has enough healthy food to eat, just as nature planned".

Answer this question yourself in two lines, a few words (all positive) and then we'll be able to go up to the last level, the highest of the logical levels.

The mission

The mission is the role you play on a daily basis to satisfy your vision and your values.

For children and pocket money:

- What role do you play? What mission do you fulfil for you to be given what you want?
- Do you do the housework for your mother, do you clean the windows?
- Do you wash the car? Do you do the shopping for an elderly person?
- Do you mow the lawn?
- Who do you help or what do you do?

Give the younger children small and easy things to do like putting away the CDs. Give them the impression that what they do is really helpful and that they deserve what they get. Of course, birthdays are not included in this.

Money must be earned, otherwise you have no identity. You are nobody.

Parents give what they can (accommodation, food, clothing, care and attention) and children what they can respectively (which is rare). If it is the other way round, the children think they have a right to everything. When a child does something to earn the object of his dreams, this reinforces his identity, his value is satisfied, he becomes responsible and he believes in it. Lower down in the levels, he is proud and pleased with himself. Lower down still he finds the capability, lower still he adopts the appropriate behaviour and he is the one who creates his environment. Making young people's dreams come true for them makes them blasé, lacking in self esteem and as they have no identity they end up despising the environment as well as their own lives.

Have you ever seen builder's sons who help their fathers build houses? Have you noticed that they don't take drugs?

Let us stop educating those who are always taking. I have known parents who gave their children money when they passed their high school exams. This is ridiculous. Not only have the parents enabled the child to study but they also pay them on results.

Who are the exams for? Who will have a future? The child of course! It's the child who should be celebrating and be giving his parents a gift, saying: "thanks both of you, you have enabled me to study, my future is there before me, this is a great gift, I'm very happy".

Teach your children to be proud of relying only on themselves to get what they want. If they get used to this when they are young, they will acquire the belief that they can achieve great things and will always want to go further.

After defining your vision, it is the right moment to discover your mission in the world.

People who want to change job, find their way or go into something new, should answer the following question: "what small contribution could I make to a world that would go in the direction of my vision and be consistent with my values? What could I do to help people experience what I say in my vision whilst respecting my values?"

If the role you play in life is consistent with your vision and values, you will succeed perfectly well. Only the aims and objectives that are consistent with this mission will be powerful motivators.

For the young man who spoke about fish and respecting the ecosystem, I simply asked him: "what could you do in your life that would stop fish eating artificial food and respect the eco-system?" He realised he could open a shop selling exotic fish, breeding fish, making them happy and following his true path.

What became of the architect? What could he do to contribute something to the world in relation to his vision of "everyone having enough healthy food to eat, just as nature had planned"?

He borrowed some money to create an organic restaurant that would also be a meeting place and conference venue with a library area and the sale of organic food. He understood why it had been so hard for him to succeed as an architect. It wasn't his vocation, his true mission. Today, he is a great success and of course has stopped drinking.

Any mission, even the simplest, which is consistent with the words of your vision, will be a success. When you don't have the necessary resources in a particular field your brain can acquire them.

In the town where I live, every time a new mayor is elected the run-down gym is repaired and renovated, i.e. the environment is improved for the teenagers. This is intervention at the lowest logical level. It would be much better to broaden the teenagers' values and help them satisfy these values by themselves, to check on their beliefs, modify them, define a vision and then entrust them with repainting, renovating and looking after their stadium. The older ones could do this with the help of the younger ones. There would obviously be much less vandalism because they would then take care of their work. Such experiments are being tested out in a few difficult neighbourhoods and have proved quite successful.

Give young people a role to play, a mission to fulfil.

How lucky I was to have been brought up by a father who never gave me what I wanted. Every year we wrote a letter to Father Christmas and we put it in the fireplace. My father replied by smearing the letter with soot to make us believe that Father Christmas had been down the chimney and we were happy. But when I asked for a doll I got a pigeon shoot. This was certainly a metaphor. I asked for one thing and I got another. Strange! Frustration is a technique I learned in Ericksonian hypnosis. The dream never dies because as it has not been fulfilled, the desire increases.

Imagine a boy who goes past a shop window. He sees a toy and really wants it. But his mother says: "no it's not your birthday I can't buy it for you". The next week he goes past the same shop, says the same thing and gets the same answer. He is frustrated at not having the toy. Finally, his mother buys it for him as a surprise but gives it to him a long time after. When the boy finally receives the toy it will be very important for him. If his mother had bought it for him on the day he wanted it, he may well have left it in a corner of his room and not played with it.

Your joy is tremendous when you finally get what you want after years of waiting. I bought my first doll for myself, it was the most wonderful gift I ever had. My son Benoit bought me the second one and now I have some very beautiful dolls. Frustration creates excitement about the future and the value of things.

It is essential to have dreams. If the environment makes them come true for you too quickly and if you have played no part in it, your identity will gradually diminish, your self esteem will take a drubbing and you will begin to believe that your dreams are satisfied by others. You begin to be dependent and gloomy.

My father used to force me to work to pay for my holidays in England. I didn't understand because he could afford to pay for me. At times I hated him. I worked in a supermarket filling the shelves with tinned foods. I was responsible for my holidays. I had a friend who had better connexions. She used to sit down most of the time, wrapping cheese in transparent plastic film using a machine. I thought this was great fun and she let me do it from time to time. As for me, my hands were black. When I studied "synchronicities" I understood the message that came through loud and clear "preserving makes your hands black and dirty". Let's throw away all our old ideas and old things, let's keep nothing. Throw out the old and bring in the new.

One day my father made us repaint our bedrooms. He had taught us to protect the floors and the electric plugs. We could choose the colours we wanted. Of course it took us all the holidays to do this. No-one had shown us the modern painting techniques and so paint trickled down our arms and into our hair. We were covered in it! This helped us develop our resourcefulness as well as our creativity. My sister had chosen two mauve walls and two black walls... Awful!!! It was hard on the eyes but she developed a better sense of taste after this. I chose pink all over. It felt like I was in a sweet shop. Later on, I stopped eating sweets altogether. My brother was more artistic, he painted superb frescos; swans surrounded by greenery and water lilies. He was a clever boy. It was so pretty that he never needed to repaint it! Nobody would ever touch it after that. My brother became an artist.

So we had a vision and were all fulfilling our mission which, unknown to us, was to forge our identity and satisfy our values. We were delighted. We were increasing our capabilities, adopting the right behaviour and creating our environment. My father had us live out a metaphor: "Change colour, choose the colour of your life".

My mother then took us to the market in Paris to buy cloth to make curtains and bed covers. Finally, we got to repaint our iron bedsteads.

My father always used to give us a role to play and I learned that everything depends only on me; finding out how to get what I wanted. Every Thursday he would ask me: "what's on your agenda today?" I didn't have one so I invented one. By repeating this question every week I got to be very agenda-conscious, very well organised (which is a meta program for success, procedure).

My parents went off on wonderful trips but never took us with them. They used to show us their photos when they came back and my father said: "when you get older you too will be able to afford to pay for your own holiday trips".

A friend told me recently: "I don't understand. My daughter is only 13 and she's blasé about everything. We've taken her to America and Canada, she's had some wonderful holidays. My wife gives her everything she wants, she has a lovely bedroom". Exactly! What can this girl dream about now that all her dreams have gradually come true?

When I was 18 I went through a bad patch like most teenagers. I left my parents because I was in total disagreement with my father. I hadn't finished my studies and I hadn't for one minute ever imagined being unemployed or on social welfare. I went busking in Montmartre and outside the Sacré Coeur cathedral in Paris, singing jazz and playing guitar to get money so I could carry on studying (I was after all the daughter of a great musician). I enrolled on a correspondence course in the Ecole Universelle and I worked in the day as a secretary, often staying until 9 p.m. at the office to correct my mistakes. It used to be the cleaning lady who asked me to leave. My life was hard and I worked a great deal (a 35 hour working week, what's that?). I never held my boss responsible for my mistakes.

When my father was dying I flew to Paris to see him. I realised that I had everything a woman could desire; a fascinating job, I could speak several languages fluently, I could paint, wallpaper, sow, I could manage my life and was in control of my destiny. I wanted to tell him he had given me a good education, that I was proud of him and that I loved him. But I didn't have time to do this because he died before I arrived. I think he knows now. My father didn't think about receiving love, he quite simply loved us and knew how to make us want to be the people we are. He was a great man who got us to dream without helping us make those dreams come true and this encouraged us to seek self fulfilment. He helped us understand the value of things and of self esteem.

Do not seek the love of your children at all costs. Simply love them as they are. They will obviously come into conflict with you but this will make them stronger. Try to turn them into responsible men and women, proud of themselves and full of dreams. Nourish the belief that we can do everything by ourselves. They will love you…later on in life.

Before my very eyes I had an example of "creating the life we want". My father came from a very poor family. He started work as a garage mechanic then he sold seeds in a shop. At the age of 20 he took up music and learned music theory and harmonics all by himself. At the age of 24 he played at the Paris Music Academy (Conservatoire) and won 1st prize. Twenty years later he became the choirmaster of the "Opera Comique" in Paris. He founded Music Academies in his region and passed his love for music on to his children.

My mother was a gym teacher. She had three children; my sister, my brother and I. We were still very young when she decided to improve our standard of living. She had no cleaning lady but started studying physiotherapy at the age of 40. She studied in the evening after we had gone to bed and after she had tidied up the kitchen. She courageously studied and looked after her family for five years and went on to be a physiotherapist. When my father died she started to study cranial osteopathy. She was 65. She qualified at the age of 72 and worked in my practise until she was 80. Meanwhile, she was also learning astrology. My parents were amazing. Each in their own way, they both created a life experience for us of: "no limits; where there's a will there's a way".

You can all change your life radically, improve and enhance it. You will notice that people who live off welfare benefits and who expect recognition from others despise themselves and project their own limitations onto their relatives or onto society. When what you are doing isn't right for you, do something else. This is a presupposition of NLP that seems quite simple. Put differently, if you don't get a feeling of happiness from what you are doing, change. To do this, you must accept to climb up the rungs of the ladder and above all you must accept that learning takes time. Never be satisfied with what you know or do. Always do more of the same thing. Broaden your knowledge and your map of the world.

Many men and women would find work if they knew how to work or would accept to enhance and improve their skills. Do not rely on outside help to pay for training either. Again this would mean the environment is providing you with your values of security, skills and money. It is by doing low paid and menial jobs that you'll eventually be able to afford to pay for your training.

When my children were small I used to serve breakfast in a hotel and put away the sheets. I sung and played guitar but I never stopped studying. I managed to pay for my education without any alimony for my children. Necessity is the mother of invention. You can go a long way. Go way past your mental limits. The main thing is to play your own role in an ecological way.

The proverb "God helps those who help themselves" is very true. Courage is a fantastic value that gives so much in return.

You're under no obligation to be satisfied with what you have. Don't say: "I've got no choice". You have the right to choose your life and you have a very wide choice. You just have to want it and decide it. Don't waste your time complaining or expecting anything at all from a system. State clearly what you want and climb onto the first rung of the ladder.

An extraordinary man gave me permission to talk about him in this book. His life perfectly reflects the path through the logical levels.

His family was killed before his very eyes when he was young in Cambodia. His father, mother and three sisters were all massacred. He escaped and hid for most of the night until things calmed down. He came out of his hiding place about 5 a.m. and ran away, leaving a blood bath behind him. Hundred of people wanted to flee the country and climbed onto boats of any sort, big or small. He says he was very lucky because he managed to get onto a big boat. The small ones capsized because there were too many people on them. He could see dresses and shoes floating in the water. He arrived in France in 1973 as one of the "boat people". He was one of the "illegal immigrants" to whom French President Giscard d'Estaing gave permission to stay. He found himself in Paris in the 18th arrondissement in a big room where all the immigrants slept on the floor and nobody spoke a word of French.

This young man could have got depressed, could have waited for welfare handouts, turned to drink or become a tramp. On the day after he arrived he found work on the "first rung of the ladder". He accepted lots of menial jobs. Then he decided to become a shopkeeper but as he couldn't speak French he wrote the prices on a piece of paper for the customers to see. He was only 22 years old. Six months after arriving he was already looking for premises to rent so he could import products from Cambodia. He started his business in premises of 56m² in the 18th arrondissement in Paris and sent a lot of the money he earned to his family in Cambodia (a very win/win situation don't you think?) He didn't have any days off for over 10 years, working seven days a week.

Thirty years later he now has 650 employees and is very wealthy. He is the founder of PARIS STORE and his name is Mr. Giang.

How can we explain that a young man of 22 who has lost everything, whose parents have been killed and who doesn't speak French can manage to make a place for himself, create his own identity without expecting any welfare benefits or support? He had a Vision of himself, of life and respect for his family. He had dreams and only relied on himself to fulfil them. He worked within a win/

win framework, with a very significant bonus that you will find in the chapter on abundance.

What's more, he was willing to climb up the rungs one by one and got to the top. Well done Mr. Giang and thank you for this wonderful example of courage and determination. You have provided us with experimental proof that anything is possible and that everything I have said in this book is correct.

Now, dear readers, what would be ideal for you? What are you going to do to fulfil your dreams? What role are you going to play? For any problem you encounter, go up very quickly in your vision.

1. Have a clear vision, a dream: what would the ideal be?
2. What role are you going to play? How will you go about this in concrete terms? Ask your unconscious mind: "how should I do it?"
3. Check on the usefulness of your beliefs, are they positive? Is what you areon the usefulness of your beliefs, are they positive? Is what you are doing consistent with your values? Make sure your values are simple, accessible and that they depend only on you. What other values could you add and satisfy? Values you don't have but which would be very useful such as humour, simplicity, exchange, communication, sharing, curiosity, trusting your unconscious mind and for some people, courage.
4. If you fulfil your mission and play the role that suits you, how do you recognise yourself, who are you? What does this prove about you?
5. De facto, you will be happy, proud, delighted, fulfilled and so on.
6. De facto, you will have the necessary capabilities. Your unconscious mind will give you the means to this end.
7. De facto, your behaviour will be adequate.
8. And of course you will have created your own environment.

An essential condition for success is to feel right in what you do, in agreement with both your values and with the universal laws.

Love everything you do. Take pleasure in all the tasks you accomplish, even the smallest. You can invent a game. Enjoying doing things will fill you with energy (the word is the thing).

When you are in the right place, the universe opens up its doors to you and fatigue disappears. You have lots of possibilities. Keep in mind the image of your ideal (never let your goal out of your sight and keep an eye on the ball). Act as if it had happened.

Always remember that when you don't have the necessary resources to reach a goal (a limiting belief), your mind has the capacity to acquire them.

And you can succeed perfectly whilst preserving the interests of others.

Summary: when you have a thought or desire and when you entrust your unconscious mind with this thought by creating emotion, if your image is clear, precise, close and in colour, your mind will immediately look for solutions it can project into the physical world and you will experience the result. Follow the ideas that come to you, carry out your intuitions in the order they come to you (see paragraph on "Image Techniques").

- Mission (I play the right role)

- Vision (consistent with my dreams)

- Identity (I therefore have a strong identity—this proves I am who I want to be)

- Belief (useful, appropriate, oriented to change) value (satisfied by myself)

- Which gives rise to feelings—emotion (happy, contented, excited, joyful)

- Which gives rise to capabilities (multiple, new)

- Which gives rise to adequate behaviour (transformed, illness no longer has any meaning)

- Which gives rise to environment—I create it. My life is transformed

Summary:

How to be create the life you want in six steps.

1. Write down precisely what you want (external visual).
2. Say it aloud (external auditory) and give arguments.
3. Enjoy feeling what you would feel if you already had it (create the emotion).
4. Do a PREM.

   It is **precise**: I know what I want, I am able to define and visualise it.

   It is **realistic**: I know how to go about it in concrete terms.

   It is **responsible**: I am the one who wants it, I decide.

   It is **ecological**: I totally agree with that (every part of me agrees).

   It is **measurable**: I give myself a realistic deadline; in one year to the day, in six months to the day, in X weeks to the day I will have or will have done this or that.
5. Click (look) up to the right for right handed people, up to the left for left handed. Entrust your unconscious mind with your plan or desire saying: "I really want this, (make an image and create emotion) what must I do? Thank you (be polite with your unconscious mind).
6. As soon as you have entrusted your unconscious mind with your plan, consider it done and wait. Act as if you had it and say YES to life. It will happen all by itself.

This is the 100% conviction, the absolute certainty that your unconscious mind will do what is required. Let go, let it happen. Your mind will do the rest. You don't need to consciously know how it will happen, it will happen all by itself.

To reach a target, an objective:

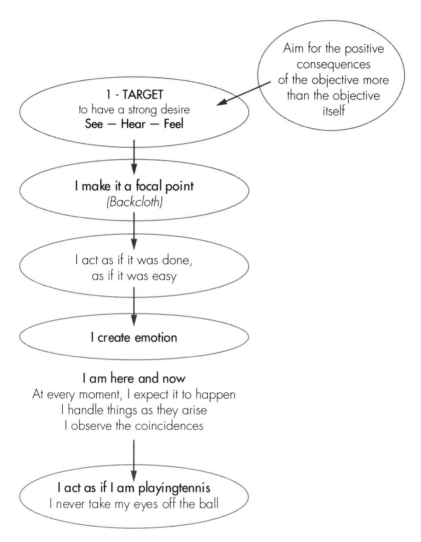

I let my mind work and it will happen by itself.
I don't even need to think about it.

For the very sceptical and for those who are afraid they won't manage, here is a great advantage; practical proof that you can fulfil your plans.

The Walt Disney technique

The sceptics will obviously think; "yes but..!" and the chronically negative who haven't even started laying out their plans are already thinking: "I'll never manage".

So, to help convince you of the power you have inside you, here is a final concept that has been passed on to us by the greatest dreamer the world has ever known, Mr. Walt Disney. He has shown us how dreams can turn into reality and especially how each of us can live out our dreams in a practical way. Robert Dilts has written extensively on NLP and had the idea of modelling the excellence of Walt Disney.

It's easy to understand how Walt Disney succeeded when we look at the way his enormous company was organised. It has three departments, just like your brain has three sectors.

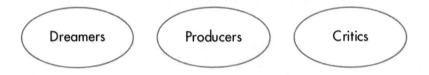

The dreamers are paid to dream, the producers to produce and the critics to be critical.

Each specialist remains in his department. A mediator passes by to collect and distribute the information.

Walt Disney knew that dreamers, of which he was one, need to be care-free and creative. Above all, it shouldn't be their job to worry whether or not it's possible to fulfil their dreams. They simply let their imagination run wild and dream.

Producers are practical people. They work in the: "how, in concrete terms, can we turn this dream into reality?" to produce something real, efficient and perfect.

Critics are not there to refuse projects, to frighten or destabilise anyone. They have hindsight and can step back to look at the dream and how to put it into effect. They are objective, constructive, positive and clairvoyant; they observe and consider things that may pose a threat to the project.

Walt Disney had discovered a vital detail. When he dreamed up "Mickey Mouse", this little four fingered, big eared mouse, it was easy to turn him into a cartoon, and he did. At this time, projectors didn't exist. Much later on, so that Mickey could be put on screen, his ears had to stay straight and stiff. By this time the producers had found some suitable material. But if the critics had said: "Yes but Mickey's ears will melt under the heat of the projectors", when Walt Disney had first drawn Mickey, he could have answered: "OK, then, I'll do something else" and Mickey would never have existed. A vital detail!

Walt Disney realised that the role of the critic is both indispensable and delicate. If the critic asks the producer: "what would you do if Mickey's ears melted under the heat of the projectors?" it is up to the producers to find a solution and when the dreamers ask: "where are you up to with the film production?" they will be told that the producers are looking for solutions and the dream goes on.

So, it was important for the critic to be able to make observations in the form of questions because "yes, but..." can cancel out some of the best ideas. As the mind only knows processes, the word "how" provokes a search for solutions.

A company that relies only on dreamers will go bankrupt. If there are only producers, they will end up "borrowing" other people's ideas because they have no creativity or imagination of their own (this happens in all fields, even in intellectual property). And a company made up of critics would be paralysed by the fear of obstacles.

Exactly the same happens between you and you. If you are only a dreamer, you want many things but you don't necessarily go into action. If you are simply a producer, you have no ideas, you copy creative people or you rely on other people's ideas. If you are over critical you stop doing things because you say "ok, too bad!"

I propose to develop these three aspects in you so you will experience the feeling of certainty that "everything is possible."

On the floor of your living room, lay out 4 sheets of paper and start having some fun.

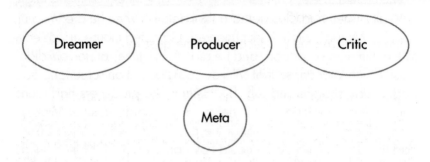

When you are in the "meta" position, you are dissociated from your 3 parts (i.e. you are a spectator).

Stand on "meta". From this position, look at the "dreamer" part of you.

Ask it: "what is your objective, your dream?" When you have clearly stated this (as you have seen above), walk onto the "Dreamer" sheet and state your desire again.

Then come back to meta.

From "meta", look at the "producer" part of you and ask: "how do you intend to go about doing this, in concrete terms?"

When you have worked out all the solutions and everything is concrete and well defined, go onto the "Producer" sheet and re-state what you are going to do.

Then come back to meta.

From the meta position, look at the "critic" part of you and ask: "can you see anything that might jeopardise the plan to…–reformulate the plan". The critic will ask the producer questions like: "what would you do if?"

From this position, everything must be seen in relation to the context. When criticism is objective and delving, go onto the "Critic" sheet and ask the "Producer": "what would you do if?"

Go onto the "Producer's" sheet and answer the critic: "in concrete terms here's what I can do" (find concrete solutions).

Then return to the "critic" sheet to see if any other comments might help eliminate obstacles or make things easier.

Each time, ask the producer the same question:

"What would you do if..?"

This is a dialogue between the "critic" and the "producer".

This little game comes to an end when the critic has nothing more to say. Once you have found a solution for each criticism, go back onto the "dreamer" sheet to ensure you are motivated by your dream, that everything is perfect and go quickly back over the two other sheets.

By doing this you will realise that anything is possible. All you needed was to balance and develop your three facets at the same time.

* * *

Well done! You have arrived at the end of this fabulous experience of creating the life you want. Simply go back to the six points summarised above. Never look at your problems or limits again, just look at the solutions. State clearly what you want. Your new life is within your reach. Don't forget to go up the steps one by one, split significant things up into small tasks and keep your eye on the ball. Don't let your goals out of sight and you will reach them.

In everything you experience in life, even the most unpleasant things, always look for the useful function because there is one. To help you with this, read the chapter on synchronicities.

Have a great life and a great journey.

CHAPTER VI

THE LAWS OF ABUNDANCE

Now we'll take advantage of everything we've learned about thought and the brain so we can relate it to the value: "Abundance". You will need to respect certain laws nevertheless and these will complete our savoir faire. In modern theories on mathematics and physics, science meets up with religion. Spirituality is at the heart of all thinking and Einstein said: "without religion, science is shaky and religion without science has no visibility".

"**Abundance**" does not mean waste and what is unnecessary, but respect and measure. We find it at any level; in spirit, in friends, in education, money etc. But money is still an inaccessible and special value for many people, difficult to satisfy—a problem of our century...of all centuries. It is the subject of much debate, bickering, pain and writing.

How do we live in abundance? This runs very much in parallel to creating the life you want, described above. Here are the main points:

First point

We know that everything in life depends on the thoughts we choose to keep in our mind and on the effort we put into changing our system of beliefs. We have seen that thought creates (thoughts are magnets). The word also creates and, over the years, our unconscious mind is impregnated with the information we have given it, recording it, seeking out solutions and thereby creating our destiny. Consequently, good luck or bad luck doesn't exist. You create your life at every moment. Think in terms of possibilities rather than in "I'm fed up" terms. Be careful! Focused thought is like a laser beam.

Any time you are in doubt, think about the wonderful simplicity of Mozart. **True genius lies in simplicity.** Success is much easier than you think.

External circumstances do not have any real importance. You may be thinking: "that's easy to say. I still have to keep my feet on the ground. As things stand, I don't see how I could possibly earn more. I've got no qualifications, I've got no money in the bank and I'm unemployed."

This is exactly what my partner Thierry said when I met him. "I don't see how I could earn any more money. I have a fixed income each month."

Obviously, this way of thinking seems logical. The only hitch is that it is precisely because of this thought that you are in the situation you are in. External circumstances have nothing to do with it.

Everything you live, either in the field of romance, your private or professional life, is the result of your ideas, of what you believe. Your unconscious mind has found the appropriate solutions and fulfilled its role, that's all. Everything is a question of attitude in the face of events (see "Behaviour Generator" in the chapter on "Tools"). Life is as we see it.

For example, a young man worked in a bank which was taken over. Everyone kept their job and the same salary. The young man complained that the increment scale had changed and that he had lost his seniority. Other people had been promoted and not him.

I asked him: "did you want to become a middle manager?" "No, not necessarily," he said. So the difference between him and the others was that they wanted to be promoted to managerial level but he didn't. He hadn't even realised that he'd been kept in his job with no reduction in salary. As he had no ambitions, what else could his unconscious mind do?

- **To succeed, don't give yourself a choice. Put yourself into the situation.** Bruce Lee always said: "don't wait for money to come to you, prepare yourself to become rich."

Act as if you had what you need and go into action. If you were sure of earning 4,300 $ (2 700 £) a month, you wouldn't have any second thoughts about buying a piece of furniture or clothes you like. If you hesitate it means you have doubts. We will see later how and when you can buy what you want.

At first, you need to set up appropriate behaviour and beliefs. Begin by believing you can become wealthy and then desire this with all your might. Be totally convinced that the solution exists and leave no room for any doubt.

It's like the stolen letter of Edgar Poe. This is the story of a letter that the police were searching high and low for, whereas it was in front of their eyes all the time. It was the mental limits of the police that prevented them finding it. They quite simply didn't expect to see it where it was.

How much (of your time and energy) would you be prepared to give in order to succeed?

This is one of the questions I ask young students. Too many people wait for things to fall into their lap. "How much are you prepared to invest to live affluently?" The ideal moment to go into action is now.

Let's look at a wonderful theory: **"Being in harmony and where you belong"**.

First of all, enjoy what you do.

One of the first conditions for success is to enjoy your job. People with a job they don't like are doubly penalised. Not only do they dislike their job but they don't earn enough. Most people live within this paradox because they are not familiar with the laws of success and they are afraid. So they cling to a mediocre security believing that affluence is reserved for others. What a strange idea!

Do you know this maxim: "character = destiny?"

If you strengthen your spirit and your character, circumstances will adapt to your desires, you will create your destiny and your life (as you have already understood) by fixing an objective. You dominate your own life and, contrary to what you often believe, it is you who have control over the circumstances.

At first, as the word is the thing, you can use and repeat this expression by Emile Coué: "Every day and from every angle, I am better and better" (this will stop you complaining).

Use the technique you learned in the logical levels (vision-mission) to discover your real mission and help you find a job that suits you better. Fix yourself a realistic deadline. You can study in the evenings or at weekends to improve your skills in any field. The aim is to enjoy what you do, do it well and help others. This is one of the secrets of abundance. At any age you can grow intellectually, improve your skills, study, gain promotion at work or change direction.

Second point

Life gives you exactly what you ask for and this is why you must start by asking for exactly what you want.

Someone said to me recently; "Madame Noël, I'm not asking for much!" Well, her mind has given her exactly what she wanted…she hasn't got much. If you don't ask for much you won't get much. Your unconscious mind will give you exactly what it has understood (if you haven't asked it for anything) or exactly what you told it, nothing more, nothing less. You must know how to ask (the PREM will be useful here).

We're going to use the VAKOG—see, hear and feel. In the same way as when you determined an objective, write down on a sheet of paper precisely: "How much do I need to live each month?" Precision is the main quality required here and the fact of putting it down in black and white with amounts and deadlines will be the first step towards big change.

When we don't know where to go, there is a very good chance that we'll go nowhere. It is the same where money is concerned.

How much do you want to earn and how long do you give yourself to get to that figure? The first condition is to write it down. People take quite a long time to answer when you ask them how much they want to earn next year, how much they deserve or how much they think they are worth.

They're unable to answer on the spot. How can you expect your unconscious mind to give you anything at all if you don't know how much you want?

Wanting to live affluently is too vague (it's general). Be precise in what you want. Write clearly on a piece of paper the amount you need to live comfortably (plus your intention).

On the same page, make a list of all the costs and overheads that justify earning this amount of money. Do not forget a house cleaner, the hairdresser and small gifts for your family. Go into detail (be specific) as this is the "precise" parameter of PREM.

Now, you are going to concentrate on yourself. On another sheet of paper, write down what you think you can earn. This is paramount. Write down the figure that comes to mind. You should think of the amount you think you're able to earn. Fix your deadline at one year. In one year, to this day, I want to be earning this much.

The figure you have written represents exactly what you think you are worth and a figure will be inaccessible for you as long as you continue to believe it is inaccessible. Why not enlarge the image you have of yourself in an instant? Now try writing down a figure that is much more satisfying for you.

Put this piece of paper with the amount you need to live comfortably on a shelf or a piece of furniture, along with the list justifying that amount. This concerns your everyday life.

On a third piece of paper, write down everything you would like in life. To succeed in life you have to start by dreaming (Vision).

- A car, what specifically?
- A house, what specifically?
- Plastic surgery, what specifically?
- Helping the children, how specifically?
- And so on

No need to underestimate. Remember that the notion of "difficult" or "easy" doesn't exist for your unconscious mind. Making out this list will enable you to measure how broad your mind is. If you were to give this list to certain rich people they would be very disappointed at having to restrict themselves to what you have written.

People who live in houses worth several million dollars and have servants, horses, swimming pools and tennis courts find nothing extraordinary in their standard of living and sometimes even think they're not happy enough. This is quite simply because they have no mental limits and for them anything is accessible because they believe it to be so.

So make a list of all your dreams. At the top or bottom of this list, write: in 7 years, to this day, I will live in abundance. This idea will become part of you and will impregnate your unconscious mind.

I can imagine many people already scratching their head and saying: "There's no way I can become affluent in 7 years. Doing what and in what field? And how can I convince myself I can become affluent because I have got nothing?" Well, use the same technique you used to convince yourself that you could not earn more, that you've used for years: repeating words and going over and over the same old thing. Wanting something has no meaning if you don't believe in it. Everything is in your thought. The stronger your thoughts, the quicker they will appear. Go back to the drawing of the target (Chapter IV) and follow it. Strong desire (the creation of emotion) gives strength to thought.

Every time your mind is slowed down by a problem, you push affluence away. Think in terms of "solutions". **Entrust your unconscious mind and your energy with your problem and believe that it will sort it out. It will solve itself. Let it go.**

Think in a calm and collected manner about what you want. Don't feel guilty if you have negative thoughts. You are only human and you are not used to trusting your unconscious mind. Refer to the chapter: "Toolbox" and simply read the "thoughts technique". Your negative thoughts will go away all by themselves.

Imagine I come to your home, I ring but you don't open the door. I ring and knock but you don't open. I knock louder and louder and still you don't answer. What do I do? I don't knock down the door, I go away. It is the same for a negative thought.

Someone told Winston Churchill that the Normandy landings could have been a disaster. He answered: "Of course it could have been a disaster. There are two types of people. We will always have negative thoughts because we are human. There are those that take thought as being the truth and act accordingly. I am in the second category: I take that thought, throw it out and forbid it to come back." The technique you will find in the chapter "Toolbox" is different, efficient and very easy. You can also act like an ignorant child with regard to a negative or undesirable thought. Smile and give it a counter-example (genius lies in simplicity).

Have you noticed that it's your imagination acting inside you? You can do so much with your imagination! You can use it to create anxiety, problems and so on. Use your imagination to change your thoughts and create a new image of yourself.

If you want to turn what you have written into reality, tell yourself that if other people have managed to earn the quantity of money you are dreaming of, then why can't you? Entrust your unconscious mind with this request in a loud voice. It will send you ideas. Follow your intuitions. You will be surprised to discover that your unconscious mind easily manages to do what you cannot do consciously. This means that the solutions it finds for you will always be in your best interests and those of others. Remember this presupposition of NLP: "we are perfectly capable of succeeding whilst at the same time preserving the interests of others". Your unconscious mind is an expert in this field—ecology—let yourself be guided and dance with it.

Be responsible for your own objective (internal frame of reference). Don't use other people's failures as a reference because if you study the path they've taken based on their PREM, you will see that their objective wasn't precise or realistic enough. It may not have been ecological and not even measurable. In short, they may have been unable to fix an objective or what they did wasn't consistent with their vision. Don't let yourself be influenced by a friend with money problems. His story is not your story. Don't buy into the problems of a crisis otherwise you may well get caught up in it.

You don't need your own money to succeed and don't count on other people's ideas.

Now the deadline: "I'm giving myself a year. In one year to this day, I'll earn this much. In two years to the day, in three years to the day..." Make plans.

Third point

Auto-suggestion: use the power of words and circumstances to obtain your desires. Certainty is acquired by repeating words.

For example: "each $ or £ I spend returns to me tenfold. The universe is plentiful and I am part it. A fair portion of this abundance is reserved for me and I now lay claim to it". Recite this with conviction.

If you go to sleep every evening to the sound of the words: "success, wealth, health, happiness, peace, love, harmony," I would be very surprised if you wake up in the morning to the sound of: "poverty, mediocrity, horror, illness".

Don't think about excellence in order to reach it. Bring together all the conditions for learning, for improvement, patience, simplicity, challenge and the pleasure of doing things. This is the path to excellence.

In order to have money you have to stop thinking about it, but this is all some people do. You simply need to want to improve a group, a system, to do a favour, to like what is beautiful and clean, to love what you do and you will receive money. The most important is your goal, your intention. Give this intention to your unconscious mind. But don't tell it what to do. Simply impregnate it with the desire. As it is extremely sensitive to the power of words (in the beginning was the verb), you can influence it with words at will.

You now know that auto-suggestion plays an important part in your life. You will live affluently when you have convinced your unconscious that you are able to live in such a way. Just as some people have convinced themselves they can't live without welfare assistance. Everything you keep repeating to yourself will happen. When the conscious mind comes into conflict with the subconscious, the safest way is repetition.

Autosuggestion can be verbal or visual. Explain to your children why it is important to tidy their room. You know how to ask them but they don't see the point as they will get everything out again the next day. The more the unconscious mind sees an image of disorder or dirtiness, the more it will create such conditions in the future so as to live in untidy and dirty conditions. Their lives will be the reflection of their room because the mind is impregnated with the image. This is auto-suggestion.

Fourth point

Creating the context for Affluence: open an account in 3 different banks; one account that your salary is paid into, another for your savings and a third for providence. You already have one account, put 20 $ or £ on the two others (here we are applying the "as if" method).

Take 3 notebooks—red, yellow and orange (not green) and update them regularly. If you like figures, figures will like you. Be clean and well-organised.

DATE	TRANSACTION	CRÉDIT	DÉBIT	BALANCE
12/08	Cash deposit	20 $ or £		20 $ or £

On the cover of these notebooks write your family name, first name and your bank account number. Love your book, pass your hand gently across the cover and say or think "together we're going places". You have just created the context for affluence. Keep your notebooks updated regularly and your unconscious mind will do the rest. Necessity will create the means. The more you love figures, the more they will give you.

Fifth point

Loving the value and knowing how to develop it: money is a value which is neither bad nor good. Like all the other values, it depends on the explanation you give to it and on **your intention**. A value is a force that you use in the way you see fit; positively or negatively.

If you water plants too much, the roots will rot. If you don't water them at all they will die. When you know how much water to give them they are so beautiful. Sometimes they will appreciate a fertilizer and of course they need care and attention. It is exactly the same for values, of which money and abundance are a part.

It is perfect if your intention is ecological. For example, providing your family with pleasant accommodation, wanting to grow intellectually, helping others and making life safe for ourselves is commendable. Being at the right place in the universe opens doors for you.

The opposite of fear is love. A boy who loves a dog is not afraid of the dog and the dog gives the boy love in return. A racing driver who loves risk, speed and his car is not afraid either. Base your decisions on love rather than on fear.

The value will give us the love we have for it in return. If you love courage, then you have some. If you adore love, then you have some. It is the same for money and abundance. There are people who are afraid of money or who have a bad opinion of it. Any value will be good or bad depending on your definitions and on the way you develop them.

To live in abundance you may need to change the way you satisfy the values "success and money". We've seen with the logical levels that a value cannot be given to us by others. So, get out of the unemployment spiral and enjoy doing any menial job you can before you find your true place. Do a good job and help others. Do not count your hours. This is one of the main causes of job insecurity and it proves you don't really like your job. The 35 hour week set up by the government in France fosters mediocrity and narrow-mindedness. The important thing is to remain ecological with regard to your family and yourself but don't forget your leisure activities. Don't start coming home very late in the evening. Whatever you do, do it well and take the interest of your company to heart because it is providing you with the money you need to live on.

People are very concerned about what a company should give its workers. But what do the employees give the company? How can any country have roads, schools, nursery schools etc. without active people who don't mind working long hours, paying enormous social charges to support those who feel they are badly done to?

The more taxes a company pays, the greater part it plays in the life of the community and the more it prospers as the universe opens up its doors to it. If a company makes a profit this means it is healthy. Rather than envying it and attempting to reduce its earnings, become active yourselves, enrich others through what you do, work with pleasure, to the best of your ability and you will get richer.

It's never too late to do the right thing. What you haven't done until now you can begin doing today. You will often have to agree to start at the bottom of the ladder and work your way up, each time earning the amount that matches your knowledge (you can often climb very quickly).

When I started looking for a new secretary I soon realised that many job seekers cling to the skills they have used in the past instead of opening up and being keen to go into a new future that is different from what they did in their previous job. They don't try to evolve and improve themselves.

If they had attempted to discover which values they could contribute to a group, they would have been much wealthier long ago. This is what successful women have managed to do: improve their skills, become richer and adapt to new technology. We need to give in order to receive and to enjoy investing or throwing ourselves into things.

I wanted to work in Italy, so I learned Italian in three months using a CD, a book and 15 minutes a day. It cost me exactly 37 $, meaning that learning doesn't have to cost a lot. We simply need a goal and to be motivated.

Other people have spent years studying and end up unemployed. Maybe their objectives were not very precise, realistic or responsible. Were they really in the right place with regard to their choice? The ability to recognise our mistakes is one step on the path towards learning and success. It isn't failure. It is a result, feedback.

Observing and accepting that the world is changing, that sometimes we need to make considerable efforts to adapt and question ourselves, has nothing to do with failure. It is a challenge.

In this case, it will be of paramount importance to redefine your mission and vision. Then go over the 5th law of success explained the chapter: "Toolbox" i.e. adapting, getting around things, being flexible and going off in a different direction to succeed. Don't hold the entire world responsible for your choices or your state.

By defining precise, clear, ecological objectives and using the power of words, you will take control of your mind and consequently of your destiny. You can influence your life in any way you want. It is simply a question of deadline if you love what you do.

Let go of the past. Here and now, ask your unconscious mind for what you want and work with it to create something new. Tell yourself you've played and lost. You've invested but lost your initial investment. Let it go without regret. What you'll obtain in the present will be much more powerful. Play fairly and don't waste your time being angry with others. We will see later that life punishes those who deserve it. It is better for you to tune into the wavelength on creating a new life and let the universe look after the rest.

Let us go back to the values technique and use it with abundance or wealth.

a. "What do abundance and wealth mean for me?" Give a simple and accessible explanation, e.g. having no qualms about buying what is necessary, justified and deserved.

b. "What is my intention?" e.g. to improve my comfort and that of my family, to study and help relatives who are in need (win/win).

c. "How do I intend to go about this in concrete terms?" By fixing myself ambitious and realistic goals. By improving my skills. By putting the best of myself into what I do. I can add a few skills to my collection, provide quality and service, fix realistic deadlines, improve my life and that of others.

Then let your unconscious mind find the many ways of turning this into reality that it will subsequently make known to you.

Sixth point

Concentrate on what you want. Concentration is another key to success in many fields. When you've reached a good level of concentration, your ability to find solutions (hence to solve problems) will become amazing. It is not by hating life in poverty that you will live in abundance because you get what you concentrate on. **Concentrate on what you love so as to attract it to you.** When you start a business, you must concentrate very hard on your goal to succeed.

Here is a little exercise on concentration. When you have defined on paper exactly how much you need (i.e. the amount you want to earn), the deadline you have fixed to get to that figure and the list of everything justifying it, try this: take a shiny object or a flower whose centre you can see. This will be a good opportunity for you to buy flowers every week. Go and sit down and concentrate on the centre of the flower, without moving, for several minutes per day. Stare at the centre and empty your mind of all other thoughts. Obviously, after a while, you will no longer see anything, or maybe a halo. Then think only about the centre of your flower and when the only thing you can see is this centre, repeat this sentence of Emile Coué: "From day to day and from every angle I am better and better. Calm down, I am in control of my destiny" (for about 5 minutes).

You will find the seven laws of success according to Herbert Armstrong in the chapter: "Toolbox". In the universe, there are seven constant laws. If just one of these constants were to vary in the slightest way, everything would be different. The seven laws already existed at the time of the Big Bang. "The ultimate principle of awareness containing the intelligent recipe for conscience, whilst also being the provisional location of the number of probabilities." (God). You cannot visualise an ultimate principal but you all have one inside you. Consequently, we are all God.

A legend tells that at one time all men were Gods. But they took advantage of their divinity so much that the master of all the Gods summoned a council which was to decide on the ideal place to hide this divinity. Some said: "We can hide it in the depths of the earth". Yes, but man will dig and dig and will get his divinity back again. Someone else said: "Let us hide it at the top of the highest mountain." Yes, but man will climb and climb and will find it. "Let us hide it at the bottom of the ocean," said another. Yes, but man will dive deeper and deeper and will find it in the end. So where shall we put it?

A child was passing and said: I know where to put it. In a place no-one will ever think of looking." And to this very day, men have been digging, diving, climbing in search of something that is inside themselves!

This is why, when you have seen the centre of the flower and emptied your mind of thoughts, you can repeat: "From day to day and from every angle I am better and better. Calm down and know, I am in control of my destiny." The ultimate principle is not something or someone on the outside that moves the world with a magic wand. You are the one who can bring about total change in your life.

"God helps those who help themselves". Use the power of words and broaden your mental limits (you can stop complaining, criticising and waiting for outside help). **ACT!!**

Give a positive welcome to others in your mind, i.e. presume that people will be nice with you and they will be (the belief influences the environment).

Concentrate on what you want. When the spirit becomes powerful the word becomes an order and the time lapse between assertion and fulfilment is increasingly short. Then, as James Redfield says in "The Prophecy of the Andes", a coincidence happens.

When your spirit has become strong and self assured, you will realise that existential problems no longer have a hold on you. You will understand that things are only as important as you think they are. Nothing exists without energy. Don't put your energy into useless things. Let go. The value you give to an event makes it important. Don't put any value into negative things. Remember that people have only one mental access code in their head to do what they do (no victim, no-one guilty). They cannot do otherwise.

A problem is only a problem if you think it is. If you accept what is happening whilst looking for solutions and the useful function of the problem, you will experience long- lasting peace.

When you observe a sky darkened by clouds you can't see the intense light of the sun. But above the clouds the sun is shining. The problems in your life are like clouds. You can solve them but others appear. "What have you concentrated on in your life?" The most beautiful thing after the rain is a ray of sunlight shining through the clouds, lighting up the dark and melting the ice.

By concentrating on the centre of a rose or daisy you will discover the path that leads above the clouds, where the sky is always blue. Don't waste your time trying to blow the clouds away. Entrust your unconscious mind with your problems, look for solutions, change your vision and concentrate on the words and images of your desires.

Seventh point

Changing our mental limits as these are the greatest obstacle to success. Let's go back to this notion of mental limits. By broadening this limit, you broaden your life. Consequently, check that your goals are: ambitious, within your reach and able to broaden these limits."How do we get to know our mental limit? "

Regarding the sum of money you consider you need to earn, the figure you've written down represents what you **think** you're worth. Hence, it is a reflection of the image you have of yourself and therefore of your mental limit. No-one becomes wealthy if they don't believe they can be.

It is important that the internal, subjective image you have of yourself should be the image of someone living in abundance. The figure you have written down is the most you **want to earn** but certainly not the most you **are able to earn.** How can we explain that some people get to this figure in one month, others in one week, others in one day and others never?

Examine the belief you have about money. If need be, change it totally. If you have now written a higher figure on your piece of paper, you have already started to believe in it and to have a new self image.

Lay down a plan for progress on paper (external visual) by writing: "In one year to this day, I will have doubled what I've got. In two years to this day, I will have tripled it. In three years to this day I will live in abundance."

This thought must be part of you and live with you. Until now you have been very good at convincing yourself of the opposite! The stronger your thought, the more quickly it will become reality (have another look at the technique: "Monitor your beliefs and reach a target", Desire + Emotion).

Obviously there are certain rules to be respected and this will make all the difference.

Eighth point

Let us now turn to the laws of abundance. We will check that everything I have said in this book is correct and corresponds to the universal laws.

Global Man

The dots represent the moments you throw yourself away from the centre, when you are not where you belong, and you receive a blow from the universe.
The dot outside the circle means you are dead. It is too late. You will come back another time.

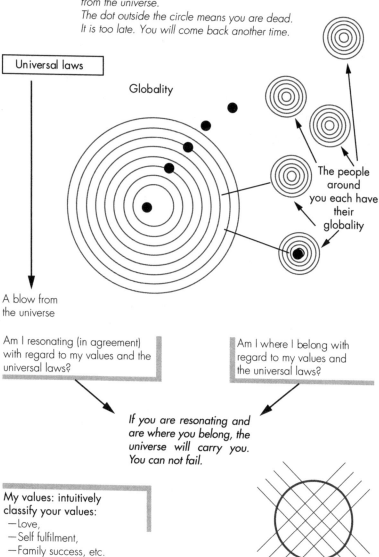

Universal laws

Globality

The people around you each have their globality

A blow from the universe

Am I resonating (in agreement) with regard to my values and the universal laws?

Am I where I belong with regard to my values and the universal laws?

If you are resonating and are where you belong, the universe will carry you. You can not fail.

My values: intuitively classify your values:
—Love,
—Self fulfilment,
—Family success, etc.

The terrestrial globe lives in a cross-ruling of telluric Hartmann waves that you can not modify. You can not modify the universal laws either.

We are governed by universal laws that sometimes we don't understand and that we are unable to alter. We don't know them in detail and some people are even unaware of their existence. Nevertheless, you somehow realise when you are doing things outside these laws, you have a sort of personal intuition.

We have come onto the earth to evolve and we must do our best to make our life a masterpiece. How are we to respect these laws? The diagram on the previous page is called "Global Man", it is your entirety. Theoretically, you should be at the centre of yourself, in harmony, in good health, with friends, in a nice home, with happy children…contented.

Your way of eating goes with you, (it's not because you eat in a certain way that everyone should eat like you). Everyone will do what they have to, (even your children will make their own choices).

Then there is the way you behave. It's not because you act in a certain way in a given situation that everyone should do the same. Each person, in their model of the world, will act on the basis of their childhood filters, their beliefs, values and evolution.

Then there is your way of thinking, of reasoning, your values and criteria. We have seen that when we have a value, we have the impression it is universal and that everyone should apply it. We don't all have the same values and in our entirety we class them in a hierarchy and they are unique for each of us.

All around you are your family and friends, your job, holidays, the dog or cat; everything you include in the entirety of your being. This is what we call global man (or woman).

Every time you are not consistent with what you are doing or saying, you push yourself off centre. For example, you go out to friends' for dinner one evening but you don't really feel like it. You're not consistent with what you are doing (you will have a little tummy upset). Using the universal laws we can check on the work done higher up with the values. How many people go to work every day not liking what they do, perhaps even hating it, and simply doing it for the money? This is a good way to be poor because they're not consistent with their ideas nor their values and work in a win/lose framework.

Every time you are not consistent with your values, you push yourself off centre, you receive a slap from the universe (metaphorically speaking) then illness, discomfort or ruin set in. Rather than protesting against the system or the company, bring yourself into question and refocus because you are pushing yourself off centre all by yourself. Remember the "action/reaction". You alone are responsible for your problems.

We should ask ourselves two questions in life: "Am I consistent (in agreement)? Am I where I belong?"

In relation to whom or to what? In relation to my values and the universal laws. The continuity of a company, health and abundance all depend on the way in which you answer these two questions.

People who succeed don't worry whether their business will make money or whether the shop or company are in a good location. They simply try to enjoy what they do, do it well and aim for quality. In this way they make a lot of money.

Bruce Lee didn't go to America to get rich. After the Korean War, he simply wanted to explain to the Americans that the Chinese weren't their enemies. He wanted to teach them about his wonderful culture. It was useful, he was very enthusiastic, he brought his philosophy of life with him and he became very rich. He was in the right place, consistent with his values and ideas.

The work you have done on values is of paramount importance because all those you prize may not depend on you alone. You will be able to live in abundance when what you are doing is perfectly consistent with your values and the universal laws.

It is also interesting to take into account the seven laws for success by Herbert Armstrong (see chapter: "Toolbox"). When you do a job badly or approximately you are not consistent with the universal laws; (Second Law: learning, being skilled). Being where you belong means providing quality.

It's the same if you open a restaurant without knowing how to cook or being an interior decorator with no taste. You need to give yourselves realistic deadlines and enjoy working in another field while you train and practise in preparation for your future job.

When are you not where you belong?

Around you, at the logical level of the environment, are your wife, husband, children, parents, neighbours and the whole world. They each have their own way of eating, thinking, behaving, their values, their criteria…their entirety. One of the fundamental laws is that you have no place in the lives of others as a whole. Your children's divorce is none of your business. Let them live their lives as they see fit. It's up to them to choose who they go out with, who they date. You can't put walls around your children.

A young grandmother who was always giving her opinion about the way her daughter in law brought up her grandson found herself crippled with pain. The day she understood that her new role was to love her children, to trust them and to stop interfering in their lives, her aches and pains suddenly disappeared. Your sole mission will be to act as trusting spectators where your children are concerned, to imagine the best for them, not to have objectives for them but to accept their tastes. In this way you will avoid stomach and intestinal problems, backache and cataracts.

Criticising is the proof that we are observing the entire life of others and you are not where you belong when you criticise. Envying someone is exactly the same. In both cases, you will get a "slap" from the universe.

You came into the world to evolve. You have lessons to learn and duties to perform. Your role is not to make other people evolve nor to do their duty for them.

As I've already said, when someone has really acted badly towards you there's no point in being angry with him/her. You can't replace the universal law. This person will receive a much more powerful slap from the universe than the punishment you would have liked to give. Instead, tune into the "constructing your life" wavelength. Observe what you want for yourself because what you send out (what is received) will come back to you twice as strong. Be neutral. Think only about your own happiness and you will live in happiness.

You are not where you belong either if you steal or copy someone else's designs or studies to make money, whether it is in music, science, objects or art. Do what you have to do, create things yourself, accept your own skills and trust in your own potential. Be different and new. Otherwise, you could earn money in the short term then lose everything.

Pay your taxes. One of the universal laws is to play along with society. People who calculate ways to avoid paying taxes will become poorer in two ways. The unconscious mind will find clever ways to avoid taxes and this is dangerous because sooner or later the universe will send them a big problem that will cost much more than taxes.

Enjoy paying your taxes. If you pay it is because you have earned. Thanks to you there will be an improvement in the environment, modernisation and embellishment. You are part of the universe and the universe is plentiful. There is a just and fair abundance reserved for you. You can stake claim to it now and obtain it. Ask for it whilst reciting this phrase intently and with conviction: "there is a just and fair abundance reserved for me and I now stake claim to this. Thank you."

You will become wealthy as soon as you stop thinking about it, when your unconscious mind has become familiar with what you think you are worth and when you enjoy doing things with good intent. Act in a win/win framework, whilst giving the best of yourself with a view to helping others and being useful.

When you buy anything, make sure it is justified or that you deserve it. It is not realistic to buy a Rolls Royce when you work in a factory, have 3 children and a wife at home. It may be if you earn more, improve your position and life style. You are "where you belong" when you deserve what you buy and when it's justified. In the little world called "The Jet Set", some people are consistent with their values: "money, beauty, dreams, pleasure" and their mental limits have exploded. Some of them spend the equivalent of a worker's monthly pay on a bottle of wine. In their world this is natural, there are no limits. This is constant pleasure that does no harm to other people. What they observe is love and pleasure: they therefore live on love and pleasure. We each have our own way of looking at things.

Living in abundance means living in tune with our own values and with respect for the universal laws.

Other laws could demonstrate abundance. Man was created in the image of the universe. Everything on high is like everything below and three key forces are internalised within him. These three forces are the three principles which are constantly creating life. We could simply say that the key to our existence is to be found in these three points.

The First force – the "will to act" law (glorious)

Now you know the Walt Disney technique, you realise that concrete action is necessary once you have had the dream. How many people hanker after so many things yet do nothing to obtain them? This first force means going from the abstract to the concrete. As soon as you go into action, everything starts moving so you can fulfil your desire.

Will-power is a force that comes to us from the ultimate principle and which makes us free beings. As soon as you put will-power into action, all external events start moving to help this force self-fulfil. This force goes very well with the value "courage" that I am so fond of. "The force of life can only be deployed in action," said Bruce Lee. The mistake we often make is to wait until we have money to decide what we could buy with it. The unconscious mind can't act without precise desires, precise needs. Define, choose and as soon as you have gone into action, the second law will immediately come to your assistance.

Don't wait until you have enough money before buying a beautiful desk. On the contrary, choose it and order it. If you really need it, you deserve the best and you will find the money you need to buy it. Don't wait until you're rich before buying a car. If you really need it and it is justified, you deserve the best. Choose it, order it and you will find the money to pay for it.

I tried this for the first time 25 years ago. I was living in Toulouse and my consultancy was in part of my house. I'd bought a desk and three armchairs in a flea market as I didn't want to over-spend. What I had bought really looked awful and I realised that if I was going to see people for several hours at a time, the least they could expect was to have comfortable chairs to sit in. What's more, this Louis XV or XVI style desk wasn't at all consistent with what I taught. So I went to a shop called Mustering where I found and ordered the perfect desk and modern leather armchairs. However, they were much more expensive. I signed the order form and paid a small deposit. Surprisingly, they told me I would have to wait 3 months for delivery.

I didn't have enough money to pay for this furniture even though it was totally justified and consistent with the profile of my profession. My reasoning, the image and my emotion obtained the rest. When Mustering called me for the delivery, to my astonishment, that very same week I received the money I needed from an insurance claim that I had completely forgotten about. Thanks to this experience, I understood how the process worked. I could write a book containing hundreds of real-life examples. When you are in the right place, the need creates the resources. Go into action

The Second Force – the law of providence (pacifist)

IIt is essential that the force of "Providence" never comes before "Action". This providential force comes into play **automatically** when our will-power is active; it enlightens us and shows us the path to success. As I explained in the "First Force", this is why you should order the car, the fitted kitchen, the furniture so as to have the money and not the opposite. Just as you need to behave as if you are well to be well rather than waiting to be well to behave as if you are.

Remember! You don't need to have money at the outset to succeed. **If will-power is not active, neither is providence.** As soon as you get the action going, everything will be set in motion for your desire to be fulfilled.

These two forces "Will-power/action" and "Providence" are inter-dependent.

Of course, when you go into action be consistent with regard to your values and be where you belong (skills, preparation, good health, perseverance, flexibility). For example, enrol for a seminar (if you feel the need) and you'll be able to afford it. Act as if you are happy and you really will be.

The Third Force within us—the law of Fate (righter of wrongs)

This force is responsible for applying the universal law set out in "global man". If you have started something with dishonest or wicked intentions that is almost illegal and with no real skills, in your own interest only or to the detriment of one or more people, this force "fate" will apply the law with rather nasty lessons to make you understand that you shouldn't have done it. It may be ruin, debt, receivership. In short…big problems.

The role of this force "fate" is to teach us to use our will-power, in line with the logic of the law. You don't have to suffer the consequences. If you do something in good faith, with a positive intention, the universe will help you, will open doors for you. You can only succeed and abundance will come all by itself.

Here is what you receive from the three forces on a daily basis:

- The first gives you total freedom. Nothing can stand in the way of your will-power.
- The second gives you a permanent helping hand in the shape of facts or coincidences. I hope you experience this and hence believe in it because you will see that what happens is a reward in proportion to the intensity of your efforts. Yes, **in proportion** nevertheless.
- The third forces you to understand the law and to respect it. Given that you are free, this freedom should not be used any way you want. Just as providence comes into play after will-power, fate also acts after the action of will-power and jointly with Providence if need be. **The law of fate never, ever acts before**. This goes to show that everything that happens to you is the outcome of an act.

Start the "action" and you will obtain "providence". One small detail; don't forget to thank the universe and your unconscious mind. Be grateful.

Very good. Now that you are where you belong and in harmony with yourself, write down: "This year I'm going to double my profit". (Profit is not income). The more you are afraid of taxes, the more your unconscious mind is afraid of profit. You must double your profit each year. As you have bank account books, your unconscious mind will find unexpected lines of credit. Every time you double your profit, you will double your means. Money makes money. It is high time to start thinking about doubling your objectives. This is a plan too. Progress is slow and every year you will make a decision based on your ambitions and your temperament. Fix yourself annual objectives.

Draw up plans and tables (specific and procedure meta-programs). Take time to dream while you are driving, cleaning your teeth, taking a shower, just before falling asleep every night because you need to dream to get rich. You must have a deep rooted desire to live better and do everything to reach that goal (don't count on the National Lottery).

When you have decided to change your life and have begun to put this into practise, see (the image), hear (the words) and feel (the created emotion), you will need to remind your unconscious mind of what it has to do because it isn't used to you helping it. You can work on the power of words so your unconscious mind will become familiar with them, by repeating the words you want 50 times every day.

Once the formula has been written down, the objective defined, the emotion created, the commitment made to yourself, you have a very good basis. Morning and evening you can repeat out loud: "every day and from every angle, I am better and better." This basic discipline will be particularly essential for very negative people who are constantly brooding on their dark thoughts.

Your unconscious mind will buckle down to its task. If you want to be more efficient, speak out loud as if you were giving orders (behaviour generator). If you feel silly, persevere with it to get over your doubts. The words you use will be part of your personality (logical level: identity). Create images and reasoning. You now know that your thoughts have a life of their own. Any thoughts that are regularly nourished will quite unexpectedly bring what is needed into your life to fulfil them.

Ninth point

You must understand that abundance is not an accumulation of wealth. It is an attitude of mind in the face of life. If, in your quest for money you lose happiness, you have lost everything. It isn't natural to be weighed down by worries. Some businessmen live with permanent stomach ulcers, diarrhoea or insomnia. When you have a problem, the best thing is to say it, write it down and entrust your unconscious mind with it. You can then immediately consider that the problem has gone and go where the sky is always blue. Create the emotion/feeling that the solution has arrived. Be confident and wait for ideas to come. Then (and I insist) act in the order in which they arrive.

You will notice that when you entrust your unconscious mind with a problem, it will take care of it entirely and you then quite simply and effortlessly carry it out.

Problem = solutions. Trust it. You now know you possess an incredibly intelligent computer that is not only connected to the universe but to all those likely to help you. Do what it asks you. It knows your future and what is good or bad for you much better than you do. Your situation can improve very quickly.

Mediocrity means not daring to do what you want to do because you're afraid of failure, insecurity or "what others will think". Live as if you were going to die tomorrow. If you were going to die tomorrow would you do what you are doing today? As far as I am concerned, if I knew I was going to die tomorrow I would do exactly the same as I am doing today: continue writing to you.

If you knew that failure was impossible, what would you do? Or, if you had thought that failure was impossible what would you have done? So go out and do it!!

Do you want to know whether or not you like your job?

If you had 3 million $ in the bank would you continue doing your current job? If you answer "no" then you don't like what you do. Except for those who have "inherited abundance", all people who have become wealthy have done so because they love what they do. At the age of 87 my mother is still working every day at her own rhythm. She could stop but she loves what she does. For her it's not a job but a passion. Many people carry on working despite being multi-millionaires because they get so much pleasure from what they do.

As you will have noticed, living in abundance requires a certain discipline. With regard to daily tasks, don't put off until tomorrow what you can do today. Such procrastination is dangerous. Your unconscious sends you ideas about what to do, tasks to accomplish. Carry them out! What's done is done and this frees up time for the next day when other unexpected things can happen. Always do a little more than you can. Like in music, tune a note slightly above the pitch. This pays off and can sometimes be very lucrative.

Tenth point

A final key to abundance is to take care of others.

The less you look after yourself, the more you will take care of others and the more you will live in abundance. Take care of your boss and have the company's interest at heart. Do a good job. Those who succeed and live in abundance don't calculate how many hours they work. Do your best to bring quality and improvement around you. Make plans, objectives and you will be respected. Be conscientious and methodical.

It takes bravery and boldness to start up a company and get it operational. Support the active population and be happy for them. In this way you will create your own abundance.

The more you are absorbed by what you do, the more you are in the here and now, the less you worry about the future, the quicker your mind will be able to concentrate on the details and the quicker abundance will come to you from many directions. The more you take care of others and do your job well, the more your unconscious mind will look after you.

Take pleasure in passing on your knowledge with pleasure in all areas: DIY, sowing, painting, music, sculpture, literature, communication etc.

Trust in life. Don't try to discover how you will get rich. Fix your objective first of all and your unconscious mind will lead you down the path to abundance. **Be patient** (realistic deadline). Thanks to your concentration, your unconscious mind will be prepared and will know when to seize the opportunity. Dare to ask, be bold.

Don't over-estimate the obstacles. Remember they only exist in your mind but it's not because you ask that everything will be given to you. Be flexible, adaptable and accept that things may be refused. The solution will come anyway.

You can now see why many people cannot live in abundance. They don't do any of these things and that's why they need a hard job and don't earn much.

What matters most is your attitude. Moreover, money is made to go round and round. He who buries it may lose everything and won't earn any more. Distribute it, make it grow and help others. You will then be where you belong in the universe.

If you stop bothering about your personal problems, it will be easier for your mind to do what it has to do. Money fits into the flow of life and is there to be multiplied. This is non-attachment.

Remember the wonderful expression by Han Solo speaking to R2D2 in the film "Star Wars": "I don't want to know my chances of success". Don't worry about your future, expect the best. Be ready.

As for books: learn how to choose them and don't let others think in your place.

To conclude, I'd like to give you an excellent principle: "evil doesn't exist for he who doesn't see it. The world is simply the reflection of what is inside. The circumstances of your life are the mirror of your inner life". You can live among criminals and organised crime but if you are on a different wavelength you will see and experience other things. Accept that the world is evolving. You can create your prosperity whatever the economic context.

When I used to sing and pass my hat around in Paris I was a young and pretty girl. I used to live alone. So many things could have happened to me as there was a lot of poverty and disreputable people. But I felt outside of all that due to my education, a sort of "Alice in Wonderland". I innocently ventured into dangerous and pitiless areas full of people I thought were friendly but who had it in for me. I only saw the positive side. I found out 20 years later that I could have come to a nasty end.

If there are no weaknesses, no regrets and no vibrations in you that attract problems or evil, then evil cannot get to you and you are not under threat.

Always maintain this principle that no evil exists and concentrate on the centre of the flower. There you will find the intuition you need to reach your objectives and get through your life. You will also find this very precious thing; **self love, love for everything you do and love for others**. This is the true secret of wealth. I could in fact have written this book in three sentences. It is your turn now. Have a good journey.

Michelle-Jeanne Noel

Thierry went on to new adventures on January 23rd 1998.

In the space of seven years he had reached all his objectives, he had succeeded. He has helped me to write this book.

Chapter VII

Synchronicities

Here, I am not talking about the theories of Jung. To my mind, in the human world a "synchronicity" is a conjunction in time and space of one event linked to another. Chance doesn't exist. Everything that goes on around us is cleverly orchestrated by the universe. The French writer St. Exupéry said that the invisible world is more important than the visible one. Everything speaks to us.

During one day you can come into contact with a number of people or events and each time there is a message. We don't necessarily see it, not at all. We'll soon get a headache or start going crazy if we look for the definition of everything that has happened during the day, the messages displayed by advertising billboards or what we should understand from what we've heard.

Nevertheless, there is a message inside everything we experience. It is in tune with what we need to learn. We often deny it, however, because we often misunderstand it, despite the message being clear.

The most curious and magical is that the message is always positive. The universe and our unconscious mind warn us, inform us or give us the means to act.

Whether it concerns small things in everyday life or great plans, the process remains the same.

Let's begin with a short anecdote from everyday life.

The very first time I really became aware of the synchronicities I am talking about was after reading "The Gardens of Findhorm". In this book a man goes off with his family to an arid area of Scotland where nothing grows, to create wonderful gardens that still exist to this day, with the help of the invisible world, (I recommend this book).

I was living in Toulouse at the time in the beautiful house I spoke about in the chapter on "Abundance" where I had set up my consultancy with the unforgettable Louis XV desk. My children used to come home for lunch. I had to be quick between midday and 2 p.m. One day I was preparing the salad when the 'phone rang. I dropped what I was doing to go and answer and then went back to what I was doing when it rang again. I did the same thing. When I had finished talking I picked up the salad bowl to take it into the dining room but dropped the wooden spoon on the floor. I moaned a little, cleaned the spoon and carried on when I got my sleeve caught in the spoon and it fell down again. Then I got angry.

My son, Benoit, who was only 11 at the time but who had often heard me talk about what I was reading said: "Mummy, maybe it's a sign". I looked at the salad and realised I hadn't put any oil in it. This was the first time I'd received a message. It may seem like nothing to you but when we take a closer look we realise that we aren't alone. Something is talking to us and putting us on the right track.

Here is another example that shows how we can be assisted (if we are attentive).

During this period in Toulouse, I used to go to Paris for two days each week, on Mondays and Tuesdays to see patients. Before catching the 'plane on Sunday evening I would prepare the family meals for two days. Jobs were piling up, I had no cleaner and I was always in a hurry. One Sunday evening I parked my car in Toulouse Airport and had to run with my suitcase. I hadn't quite timed it right. I don't know why, but something forced me to turn round and I saw the warning lights of the car flashing. What a drag! I was already late and I didn't even know where the switch was to turn them off. I turned around and walked back, moaning to myself as usual. When I opened the door guess what I saw? My car park ticket on the ground next to the front of the car. I slipped onto the front seat so I could pick it up and when I lifted my head I noticed the warning light switch.

How wonderful! If I'd lost this ticket on my return I would have searched through all my bags in vain and wouldn't have been able to get out of the car park. All I could do was say "Thank you". I didn't know to whom, but whoever it was, it was a little sign that someone somewhere was looking after me. My life was difficult and I realised I was not alone. I was being helped. I had never been aware of this before. Tears filled my eyes and I was happy.

After this, I began looking at the signs, the messages or "the synchronicities". When something that we think is unpleasant or terrible happens to us, if we take the trouble to step back a little, to observe and agree to go along with what is happening, we will become aware that everything in the universe is wonderfully orchestrated, in our best interests, even if it is not apparent to the naked eye. Our first reaction is to be unhappy, upset or angry. But inside an experience there is a **useful function** or a learning experience (a secondary advantage). If we accept this process, the experience will lead us toward an improvement in our life, a profitable change, an essential encounter or a useful message.

Later on, I left Toulouse with my family to go and live in Paris. I couldn't leave my patients overnight so I did the opposite, i.e. I went to Toulouse every week for two days to see my patients and I did this for 5 years. It was tiring, often difficult and I worked a lot. I still didn't have a house cleaner, I had my two sons to look after and my car was an essential tool for my work.

Now, here is some feedback on the useful function of an event.

My youngest son Benoit started learning to drive when he was 16 (accompanied by a qualified driver). His elder brother Sebastian was 18 at the time. Benoit sometimes (quite often) asked me for the car keys so he could have a little drive around the private housing estate we used to live on.

One day when I had friends over, he asked me for the keys promising he wouldn't go out of the housing estate (and as the word is the thing he did so). I refused a few times but then I finally gave in as he kept on insisting. In fact, he lied and went out to pick up his friend Alexander and they then drove off into town. Unfortunately, he went through a red light and crashed head-on into another car. As he had no driving licence he drove off and came back home with my car in a dreadful state, saying: "Mummy come quick, I've had an accident and I drove off".

At that time Sebastian had his own little car and we set off together to the place Benoit had described to us. Everyone had gone of course and so we went to the police station. There I found the accident victims about to make an official complaint for hit and run. Using my efficient communication techniques, I managed to get them to draw up an accident report in my name, everything was sorted out and we went home.

I was very angry. My car was essential for my job but now I couldn't use it. My initial reaction was to shout very loudly as usual. Then the idea suddenly came to me that perhaps there was a useful function in all that. I went off, sat down and asked myself this magical question:

"What is extraordinary about what has just happened? Nothing". I repeated the question: "what would be extraordinary in all that if I really wanted there to be something extraordinary?"

Two ideas suddenly came to mind. The first extraordinary thing is that the universe gave Benoit the lesson that I wasn't able to give him. Never again did he ask me for the keys to my car. He is now extremely cautious. I ask him to do the shopping and I trust him when he has my car.

The second thing that came to mind was that I often complained about the state of my car. Sebastian, who was keen to earn a little pocket money, sometimes offered to clean it. There were chestnut trees around the house and the hood was often covered in bird droppings that were difficult to get off. One day Sebastian found the solution: a scratch sponge. He tested it out in the shade on a small surface, and the car looked great. So he set about cleaning the entire hood with the scratch sponge. Out in the sunlight when he'd finished, it was a total disaster of course.

The second extraordinary thing was that I got a brand new hood. As it was, I was pleased with these two things but it wasn't until a little later that I understood the magic. The garage kept my car for one week. Every morning Sebastian took me to work and came for me in the evening. Before going home we used to go for a drink together at the bar on the corner of the street and chatted. He talked about the problems he had had in his teens, what he hadn't appreciated or accepted in his education. He also told me about his plans for the future. I explained to him how hard it had been to bring up two sons by myself and told him about my intentions. I'd been very authoritarian as I had to replace their absent father yet at the same time I wanted to play my role of mother and had got a little out of touch with Sebastian.

By Friday my car was ready to be picked up. Thursday evening was our last trip together. Sebastian said: "It's a pity Mum, it's been nice". "Yes, my big boy," I said "and we've grown closer again". Would I have been able to do that all by myself? A few weeks later Sebastian left to join the Air Force and met his wife-to-be. Those were our last intimate mother/son moments. The universe knew I wouldn't have been able to handle losing my son and I was cleverly given the opportunity to get closer and erase the problems we'd had in the past.

The universe talks to you and helps you. The way it does this is not necessarily the way you would have liked but it is efficient.

Signs related to cars are often interesting and the "synchronicities" or messages can be numerous.

One day, one of my patients had made an appointment for 7 p.m. He called me at 7 p.m., told me his car had broken down and asked me to wait for him. He arrived 40 minutes late, apologised and explained that the problem was the spark plugs. Three weeks later he had another appointment at the same time. He called me, apologetically, broken down again so I waited for him. He was very angry when he arrived and told me why: the same mechanic hadn't seen that there was a bad contact. He spoke in this way: "I couldn't get going and all because there was a bad contact". So I asked him: "how's business these days?" "Well I started up a business and I'm finding it very hard to get going" "So improve your contacts!" and that is what we worked on together.

I have checked car-related phenomena over and over again with experiences that have often been unpleasant.

A few years ago I bought myself a beautiful coat for Christmas. It was a bit long for me and I had to go back to the shop a few days later to pick it up as they had adjusted the hem. That evening I'd been invited to the theatre and I went to pick up Patrice, the friend who'd given me the invitation. I parked my car in the street where the theatre was and Patrice asked me if he could put his kimono in the trunk of my car. "Of course," I said, and I decided to put my new coat in too.

After the show, I took my friend home and just after starting off I heard the trunk rattling. I stopped and we went around to the back of the car to see what was wrong. I don't know how, but my boot had been opened and it was empty. My beautiful coat!! My initial reaction was again one of anger and I didn't take the trouble to write down a sentence describing what had happened, because at that time of night I wasn't in a frame of mind to look for any sort of "useful function".

In fact, the phrase was this: "I put my coat into my boot, it was stolen". There was nothing to interpret. The phrase was complete.

A few weeks after, two very persuasive people proposed a financial investment to us. It was so attractive that Patrice and several friends decided to invest in the operation. In fact, it was a swindle and we lost everything.

We obviously filed a complaint with the police. A short time later we were with the lawyer. I was thinking and said to my mother: "I should have listened to my car, she'd warned me. I put my coat (my savings) into the boot and they were stolen". We shouldn't have invested. The lawyer who already thought we were very careless or dreamers, came to the definite conclusion that I was a bit disturbed.

Now, here is an example of the way in which the messages that come before our eyes (visual external) can fall into an order, either to warn us, to confirm something or to guide us.

A young man came to me one day to fix some objectives for himself, to find his path as his life was a bit of a mess. After the consultation he was delighted, said goodbye and left. A few minutes later the door bell rang. He had come back to exclaim: "you'll never guess what I just saw in the street! A lorry with a slogan on it saying—'Your head in a bag'—That was it, my head was in a bag".

Whether it's an accident, a breakdown, some sort of problem, there's nothing to be interpreted. Write down what happened in your own words. Look at the sentence. The universe or your unconscious mind is warning you about something, in your best interests (either in business or in your private life).

What about the dramatic events of life if we seek to understand their true meaning? Perhaps it is our belief that is dramatic. What if things were otherwise?

Nine years ago I lost Thierry, my companion". This sentence is wrong in fact. How do I know I have lost him? Of course, at first I was in agony. We had planned to get married in July. In December we bought our wedding rings in the town of Le Mans where Thierry was born and left them with the jeweller so he could engrave our names on them. One month later Thierry died in a motorbike accident. The ambulance service took away the body. It was as if he was no longer mine. I was told I could see him the next day in the funeral parlour.

At 11 p.m. I was in the kitchen with my son Benoit. Suddenly a very strong thought came to my mind: "I have to go and see Thierry". "Impossible", said Benoit. "You can't go and everything must be locked up in any case." But this idea became so strong that I put on my coat and went off to the funeral parlour. When I arrived the light was on in the hallway. Nobody was there. I could see Thierry in his underwear laid out on a table. A young man arrived and said: "What are you doing here? You can't go in". I told him he was my husband. "You haven't seen me, I haven't seen you, I'll only be five minutes". Thierry's eyes were open. It was I who closed them. I don't think he would have liked someone else to do that. I spoke to him, reassured him by telling him what had happened, I told him that someone was going to come and get him, that I loved him and we said goodbye to each other.

How could I know that at 11 p.m. everything would be so easy, that I would be able to close his eyes?

A few days later we went to Le Mans with one of Thierry's daughters to look for the jewellers shop and get back the wedding rings. I wasn't at all familiar with the town and we didn't know where to begin. I had neither the address nor the receipt from the shop. When we arrived we looked for a place to park and the children thought we should walk around the streets and ask in all the jeweller's shops. This was no small task. No free parking spaces. We drove round and round until we found one just in front of a pedestrian street. It was a nice day. We parked the car and set off around the town. We had gone a few meters when suddenly we heard the music that Benoit had played on his saxophone at Thierry's funeral. It was a violinist who was playing at the end of the street. All five of us walked towards him in silence. An old man was playing this clear and limpid piece of music with a violin case at his feet. Opposite him on the other side of the road was a jeweller's shop. "Wait here, I'll go and ask" I said to the children. I went into the shop and gave Thierry's name "Yes Madam, this is the right shop". I beckoned the children to come in, paid the bill and we left. The violinist had disappeared. We didn't say a word and went to have a drink in the closest bar, overwhelmed and emotional.

It was unbelievable. We had visited only one jeweller's shop, one parking space was free in front of the right street, the violinist…Is the thread really cut? No.

Today I give conferences and seminars all over the world and I would never have fulfilled this mission if Thierry had stayed and lived with me. I have acquired a strength that I didn't have before, as if I were two people. We work together and I am never alone. When I look at his life, he had accomplished everything he had fixed for himself and because he departed his daughters received the money they needed for their studies, which is what he wanted. He had a role to play, elsewhere, differently.

I'd known this type of communication before. When my father died, my mother gave me his pendulum. Although he was a musician, he had a passion for dowsing. My children were very young when he died, I was a naturopath at that time and I also used dowsing.

I'd only had this pendulum for a few days when I took Benoit to a shop to buy him a pair of tennis shoes. I bent down to tie his laces and the pendulum must have fallen out of my pocket. I lost it. I was very upset.

Before I went to sleep that night I wondered whether this had any particular meaning. Maybe there was a message for me. Should I stop dowsing? And for the first time in my head I spoke to my father, asking him what I should do. I then fell asleep.

A few days later some friends invited us over. At one point I withdrew into their enormous library where the shelves stretched right up to the ceiling with books of all sorts. My eyes were attracted by a small book whose title I couldn't see from where I was. I had an irresistible desire to go and get it. I slid the tall ladder along and climbed up to it. It was a book on dowsing. I opened it up at random and read: "a dowser's pendulum must not be used by another dowser, the answers can be worthless". I had my answer and I was amazed. I climbed back down the ladder thanking my father.

My eldest son, Sebastian often spoke of his grandfather. He admired him very much and when he played piano he used to say; "it's my grandad who's helping me play". He used to put out the light and play very well in the dark. I didn't like that.

He was 17 when we came back from Toulouse to Paris. I enrolled him in the Draveil Music Academy. My father had already been dead for 11 years. Sebastian was his first grandson and he loved him very much (he never knew the others). He had founded several Music Academies (Conservatoires) and during a removal from one of them all is belongings had been mislaid.

Shortly after the children had gone back to school in September, I dropped Sebastian off as usual for his evening music lesson. His teacher was absent and the Principal said he could wait for me in a very big room where many cardboard boxes were piled up around a piano. The Academy was still in the process of moving.

My son started playing his piece when his gaze was attracted by a box that was right at the bottom of a pile. Nothing was written on it to suggest its contents. He had an irresistible urge to open it and find out what was inside. So he started by taking off all the boxes on top of it so he could get to the one he wanted. He opened the box and found all my father's belongings, his conductor's baton, everything.

Even though several people had already looked for my father's belongings in vain, it was my son Sebastian who, upon returning to Paris 11 years later, after all those years in the provinces, recovered what we were so fond of and keen to find. Isn't that strange?

Since then, I have begun studying all the latest discoveries concerning the universe. Many scientists have shown that death doesn't exist. It is merely a change in state that we cannot see with the naked eye but which exists. Nothing has been lost. "Nothing is lost, nothing is created, everything is transformed".

Everything is wonderfully orchestrated in the universe. The invisible world around us constantly helps us and sends us signals. It is our responsibility to listen, recognise and accept them.

I could give you thousands of examples and one book wouldn't be enough. I will end with an example of synchronicity that can change the course of someone's life. All you need to do is let yourself be guided and be trusting.

One day I was on the Paris to Marseille high speed train. I didn't like the seat I had been allocated in the slightest so I decided to change. I went through a few carriages and saw a very sad looking young woman sitting alone next to a window, staring at her cat in its travelling cage. I sat down next to her and said hello. Very quickly she told me she was an engineer. She'd been working on a project for several years that had worked out very well and she thought she would be made head of an operations department for this project. Unfortunately, the company had chosen a man who was older than her to take over and manage the operations. She was disappointed, disillusioned, sickened and had been posted to some godforsaken place a foreign country for four years. She was on her way to Marseille to say goodbye to her family.

She was wondering whether to resign, get a job somewhere else and stay in France. So I told her all about synchronicities and replied that people around us don't act for or against us, but they are influenced and are merely tools of our own destiny. She should go to this country, wait and see what happens. Certainly something unexpected could happen in her life that would be much better than she'd imagined.

For her, I was just someone she had met in a train. She listened to the message. I left my card with her, she felt happy to have talked about all this.

A few years later I received an email from a woman saying: "We met in the Paris to Marseille train, I had my cat with me and now I'm back in France. I would very much like to see you again." I answered her at once and we met for dinner in Paris. I saw a radiant woman coming towards me arm in arm with a man of about forty.

She had finally gone off to her "godforsaken place" and had never stopped thinking about what I'd said. After one year of work and boredom, a small school opened and a young headmaster was sent from France. They fell madly in love and got married. He organised the school. After three years it turned out that the older man who had be given the job she so dearly wanted wasn't at all suited to the post. Her Company had called her back and had appointed her head of department.

It was the right time for both of them to return to France. She had had to leave France to find the love of her life. What would have happened if she had resigned? Another life certainly, different, but our unconscious mind knows much better than us what is good or bad for us and knows our future.

Consider the messages from the unconscious and from life as being your friends. For any problem you encounter, any inconvenience or drama, ask yourself this one question:

What is extraordinary about what is happening to me?

(You will rarely find the answer. You'll have to ask yourself the question in the conditional).

What would be extraordinary in that if I really wanted there to be something extraordinary?

The answer will come to you in subtle ways. Trust in this process and in your unconscious mind.

Your life can become what you would like it to become. You are never alone. Have a good life!!

Chapter VIII

The toolbox

- Communication
  - The power of words
  - Good communication—self esteem
  - Sandwich
- Beliefs and changes in beliefs
  - Definition
  - Images technique
  - Change in belief I
  - Change in belief II

In any given situation, our attitude is based on a set of beliefs that we have about people, about an activity (work – family), about a person or about ourselves. **Change your beliefs, change your attitude.**

- Values
- Anchoring
- Behaviour generator
  - Change your behaviours
  - Self esteem and behaviour
  - How to change unpleasant behaviour
  - Four behaviours to obtain power
- Determining objectives – Summary
- Perception, an automatic phenomenon
- Mental strategies (to change our behaviours)
- The 7 laws of success
- How to eliminate a negative thought

Communication

The power of words

To quote Bernard Wœsteland: "Each word, each letter, each number has an energy equivalent. This is how the verb is transformed into vibrations and this energy message can circulate in the air around us thanks to billions of little particles that enable networks to form. Thanks to this, you have television."

Man's brain possesses numerous decoders that are located between the receivers (the unconscious) and the transmitters (the conscious).

The vibratory messages received in your brain (all the ideas that come to you) are transformed into comprehensible language. This language enables people to communicate and to exchange. But the information is transformed because it goes through several filters. This is why you should not take a piece of information as being the truth. Check it out.

An inaccurate piece of information can be passed down from one generation to another and become established as a truth.

Information transmitted by man is called language and we must be aware of its nature. It is merely a piece of information; it is up to us to check and alter our transmitters-receivers.

When we understand how the mind works, we realise that the danger is not only in the words we use. You do not communicate just by language. Your thoughts communicate as well. They provide a vibratory field called the aura.

When you have a thought, it travels through invisible networks that surround you and **strikes other individuals**. So, thought is one of the most important tools that human beings possess. A mother who is afraid for her children and who creates negative images, strikes them by sending 20,000 volts towards their brain.

As soon as you throw a stone into the water, concentric circles form towards the outside and come back twice as quickly. It's the same thing for thought: you create a force that will come back twice as strong.

This mother will be ill or will have problems and won't understand the whiplash that the universe has sent her. She thinks she loves her children but she is not where she belongs. By constantly thinking negatively, there comes a time when the cells of your body materialise the subject, the nature of your thought and you fall ill.

Hence, you choose your vibratory field, your wavelength, your frequency. Your life and your destiny are in your own hands.

Every day of your life you transmit and you reach individuals on multiple vibratory fields of the earth. You are on a channel broadcasting its song, in the same way as you tune in to France Inter, the BBC or Radio Monte Carlo.

You can now decide to transmit new programmes on a new frequency.

Good communication – Self esteem

Good communication with others helps create self esteem. The first thing to do: **Create a good rapport.**

What does this mean?

- It means creating a climate of trust and security.
- It means communicating the following message at the conscious and especially unconscious levels: "We have things in common. I am willing and able to understand your point of view".

Let's look at Maslow's pyramid.

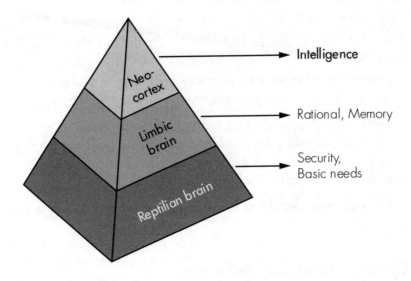

We start out at the base, the reptilian brain: security, the basic needs.

Let's imagine a boy who arrives in his first year of high school.

He doesn't know where the maths classroom is and he doesn't know where his mother will come and pick him up. He asks himself a whole host of questions. As his reptilian brain feels insecure, he doesn't listen to a word that is said in class.

Now, if the teacher takes a few minutes to introduce himself: "Hello, I am your new X teacher. My aim is to help you to…This is what is going to happen in class…" (this means "setting a frame" → telling people how things will happen). He introduces the syllabus—"from now until December we're going to…then 'till April…after that we'll have XX to do…" He then introduces the school, he plays things down. He takes an interest in the needs and the questions of the children. The pupil's limbic mind will then be able to memorise, it is rational. The child feels reassured and is able to work.

A woman arrives at the hairdressers. She gets a "hello" then nothing. If you observe her, you'll see her getting irritated, agitated. If the hairdresser, even very briefly, simply puts her fingers through the woman's hair saying "I'll be with you in ten minutes", she'll feel reassured and will wait.

It's so wonderful to have a dentist who tells you what he's going to do and keeps you informed as he goes along. "This is what I've just done, here is what remains to be done". We like to feel protected and above all to know what is going to happen.

Warning, telling, explaining, etc. This is called **setting a frame**.

If you want people to be intelligent with you, reassure them, put them at ease. Tell them something positive you have noticed about them (seen or heard).

Now, let's not forget that communication is 95% non verbal and 5% verbal.

You haven't even opened your mouth, yet the other person already has an opinion about you, he/she believes something about you. It is often wrong. Be careful how you behave, (see "The generator technique").

What do you want people to think of you when they look at you? That you are friendly, helpful, communicative, straightforward and congruent? Put these words into your brain and your unconscious mind will help you adopt the appropriate behaviour. Don't think about over-complex criteria such as "intelligent, gifted, or brilliant." You may well suffer and this is one thing that causes a lack of self confidence.

How, then, do we establish a good rapport (good communication)?

Since you arrived in the world you have seen, heard things and felt emotions. You have had educators, a socio-genetic culture and parents. You have filtered your information, adopted a system of beliefs and you have built up **your model of the world**.

Each model of the world is **unique**. We are all unique because we have neither seen nor heard the same things and because our beliefs are different. There are not people who are right and others who are wrong. There are only people who believe what they say.

All people have the right to believe what they believe, to think what they think. So, one of the first techniques you need to put in place is this: **accept the model of the world of those around you**, accept their way of expressing themselves, what they say and the way in which they say it.

We all have the right to express ourselves and you have the right to disagree.

In a philharmonic orchestra, there are many different instruments. If there were only violins or trumpets it would be very monotonous, even hideous.

You are part of the universe and you are an instrument. You have your note to play and you cannot play the neighbour's note. The guitar is important but so is the trumpet, the tuba, harp, triangle and piano: **play your note and your music score**. Be different from the others. Accept to be the instrument that you are, as well as what the others are. Accept all music scores. We can't all be trumpets, drums or violins. It takes all sorts to make a world.

You are under no obligation to agree with someone but you can understand him/her and this won't prevent you from expressing yourself.

Look for a **positive intention** for each person you speak with **in what he/she says because there is one**, or ask: "what is your intention in telling me that?" This will be more constructive than interpreting something negative. When you answer, do so in a sandwich (see the following technique).

Example: someone asks you to do some shopping for them but you don't feel like it:

Bread & Butter—"I know you're alone and that you can't get around. It's true, I have a car and I understand you asking me to do you this favour. If I were you I'd do just the same."

Ham & salad—"**Now, maybe**, today I can't because I had planned to...."

Bread & Butter—"But I understand completely, it'll be much easier for me some other time."

People do not want to be right, they want to be understood.

TThanks to your sandwich, the other person hears that you have heard. You have respected her point of view or request twice. She will take away both pieces of bread and butter and will keep what is in the middle.

First point: Synchronisation (reproduce the gestures, the words, the state of mind)

The first tool used to communicate between child and mother is mimicry and right up until the end of our lives, this will remain the best method of learning.

Synchronise, accept other people's point of view, their state of mind, their values, their beliefs.

We get on well with people who are like us.

If you go for lunch at the home of elderly relatives who don't usually leave the table before the end of the meal, teach your children to synchronise their values with those of these people. Accept their values or stay at home. When you go to France you don't take what you normally eat at home with you, you eat French. It's the same in all countries. Synchronise.

Stay "externally connected"

Observe at first and then synchronise:

- Body movements.
- Posture.
- Tone of voice (don't speak too loud if someone is speaking to you softly and vice-versa).

Maintain a positive attitude regarding yourself and others.

Welcome people positively in your mind. St. Exupéry said: "See with the heart". It's easy to get on with someone. Reflect what the person opposite you is doing. You know how to do it with very young children. Show the other person that you are interested in her.

When you reflect your children's behaviour they get on well with you. Many parents have lost the relationship with their children because of this fundamental detail.

Do not ape people. Be discreet. The person you are interacting with must not be aware of what you are doing, so get some practise.

You can: reproduce either their overall body language, part of it or cross over (e.g. the person puts their right leg on the left. You do the opposite).

One of the reasons you don't have a good rapport with others is that, very often, you are totally unsynchronised with what they are doing.

Second point: Reformulate (active listening)

During an ordinary discussion, someone utters a sentence, the other person replies with another sentence and the subject slips away. Often, someone says something to you, you bounce back and speak about yourself without reformulating what the other person has just said and you go off on your own subject.

Efficient communication means "being active". Synchronise the rhythm of the discourse with your head, focus on the other person and often say: "yes, ok, I understand. Well, well..ok" repeat what is said from time to time (the same words) i.e. reformulate what the person has just said by synchronising. Show that you are interested. You can speak about yourself afterwards. You have plenty of time.

Reformulation can be on certain words, then on every five or eight sentences. If the other person speaks quickly, desynchronise by leaning forward, for example, raise your hand a little saying: "**If I have understood you...**" then you repeat the text (same words, same vocabulary).

You can only speak about yourself or ask a question after you have reformulated. In this way, you will notice that it's difficult to listen and to remember what someone says.

I hear children say to their mother: "mummy I'm pleased, I've finished my drawing" and the mother replies: "go and wash your hands darling, it's time to eat." My darling, OK, but this is awful for the child. A boy says to his father: "I'd like to learn to play guitar" and the father blurts out: "for now, go and do your homework!"

Well done!!! Do that three times and you've lost the connexion. When the child is 15 his parents will be surprised that he's stopped talking altogether. Reformulate, synchronize.

Reformulation is magical for two reasons:

- The person feels listened to, understood, interesting, of value.
- You have understood perfectly what she has just said because it is the only way to really understand.

A math student, who reformulates the wording of a problem slowly, several times whilst writing down point by point what is asked of him, will have every chance of finding the solution.

When you give your 'phone number to someone who answers "yes", what proves they have understood? **Re-form-u-late.**

Repeat and send back the text like a wave unfurling on the beach then receding.

Of course, as with synchronisation, the person you are interacting with must not be aware of what you are doing. You will need to practise to become perfect. **It is an art** that will bring you harmony and understanding at all levels.

You will be interesting because you are interested, valued because you value others, your life will change.

The art of motivation

The sandwich technique

How to speak, get your message across and make yourself understood without offending those around you?

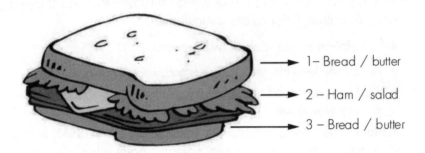

→ 1– Bread / butter

→ 2 – Ham / salad

→ 3 – Bread / butter

Bread & butter

This is your interlocutor's model of the world, her VAKO reference (what she has seen, heard, felt). Speak about her first of all and about her experience. Reformulate what she says using words like "it's true that…or…I know that". Of course, you've learned about congruence and what you say must be demonstrable and sincere. I'll give you an example a little later on. You should also use words such as: "I know it's important for you" or "what you say is important" or "that's interesting".

You accept. The other person has reasons you are unaware of and you finish your bread and butter by saying: "I entirely understand you" or "I can understand that".

Never say at the outset: "I understand" before having shown how you managed to understand. Maybe you have noticed, for example, that when people are very sad because they have lost someone or a pet and you start off by saying: "I understand", you may get the immediate answer: "what do you understand, you can't understand".

To give feedback to someone, i.e. to tell her what you think of her or of what she has done, first of all state everything good you have noticed, seen and heard. Again, be congruent. The bread and butter is **positive for your interlocutor, enhancing, respectful of his/her values.**

Speak about the other person first.

Ham & salad

Now say what you want to say, take your time. Replace your traditional "yes but" by two hypnotic words "now, perhaps". When you use the word "perhaps" you impose nothing.

Regarding feedback to a sportsman or student; after noting everything good about what he did, tell him what else he could have done or what he could now improve, perhaps what you would have done in his place, perhaps. Never say what he didn't do or did badly, but what he **could** do better.

In an ordinary discussion, the ham-salad is used to speak about yourself, about your point of view. "Now, perhaps, I believed, I thought, I would have liked and so on."

More bread & butter

Before the other person can answer, you immediately add: "but it's interesting" or "it's important", "I understand very well. In your shoes I would have done worse than you", or "I would do just the same as you".

In the case of feedback: "but it was good, you have improved a lot" or "You did that quickly" or "In any case, you went all the way". Always be congruent and positive.

When you say "yes but", you cancel out everything a person has just said. What is clever in the sandwich technique is that when you add your bread and butter at the bottom, the person unconsciously thinks that because you are using "but", that you are cancelling out everything you have just said in the ham-salad above. So the person accepts it.

If you've followed the rule properly, you've twice respected their point of view or their work and you've twice been heard to say that you understand. The person will take away the two slices of bread and butter and take what's in the middle.

To do this, you need to be very congruent and to want to help or respect the other person. This is part of the patterns of influence. Influencing in itself is not important. It is the way in which you influence that counts. In a win/win frame.

Here are two examples of a sandwich:

One of my students told me he could no longer communicate with his wife. They were getting divorced. She would drop the children off in front of the garden gate because she didn't want to speak to him any more. Of course, all this wasn't very pleasant for the children nor was it good for their future. This man had lost the relationship and I suggested the only thing he could do now was a written sandwich. To prepare him for this I needed to know a few details about his wife's life and what she blamed him for. Here is the result:

Bread & butter: "I'm currently studying communication and personal development and I've just understood some very important things. It's true that for 17 years you brought up our children by yourself. I was never there and I only thought about my job. I know, for example, that one day you asked me to bring some medicine home for our son and I didn't. It was too often hard for you. I've understood that you suffered a lot from my behaviour. I don't know if I would have had as much patience as you. I know it was impossible to talk to me and I didn't listen to you. I understand very well how you got to the attitude you have today (all of this must be congruent and the simple fact of talking in this way makes us really understand).

Ham salad: "Now, perhaps, I was too young, I hadn't learned to communicate, perhaps I wanted to give you a certain standard of living and I devoted all my time to my job as it was very important for me".

Bread & butter: "But I understand you very well and in your place not only would I have shut you out but I think I would have "slapped you" (it is excellent to do more than the other person).

This man asked his eldest son to give the letter to his mother saying: "Please mum, read dad's letter. Do it for us". And she did. A few days later he got a phone call from his wife saying she agreed to meet him. She simply wanted to be understood. This was the case because the simple fact of making a sandwich forces you to be congruent and shows you have really understood.

A young man of 17 asks his father if he can go out one evening. The father refuses, so the son answers:

> You don't want me to go out tomorrow evening. It's true that my school grades are very poor, any father would be worried. It's also true that you never see me studying and that I give you no indication that I want to improve. I know you want me to succeed in life and that you worry about me as far as alcohol and drugs are concerned. I also know that, seen from the outside, you could get worried about the people I hang out with. Now, perhaps, this party is at a friend's that you know and I could give you their phone number. I can tell you here and now that I want to pass my exams, I know my limits and I intend to improve my results at school. Perhaps I can also promise to stay sober.
>
> But I understand you very well. If I had a son like me, I wouldn't let him go out and I think I might even put him in boarding school, (do worse).

What would the result be? The father will at last have heard that his son has understood and could reply: "ok you can go out this time."

You can do things very simply. Don't say to your wife: "darling your cake was a bit burned". Tell her first what was good: "you prepared a wonderful dinner. Did you notice that everyone had second helpings, it was superbly presented and there was a nice atmosphere. Now, perhaps the cake was a bit burned but it was a wonderful meal". She will reply: "Yes, next time I won't leave it in the oven as long".

If you say to a tennis player: "No, no! I've told you a dozen times to bend your arm for heaven's sake!" he may well throw his racket up in the air and walk off the court.

Here is what you can say: "you were in the right position as far as the net is concerned (if it's true) your footwork is very good, it's

227

getting better and better." Look for the true and positive elements and bring them out.

"Now, perhaps, you could bend your right arm a bit more when you…" (Say how he could do things differently, not what he did badly).

"But you're making progress, that's good". You will hear the player say "send me the ball back", wanting to carry on practising.

Beliefs and changing beliefs

- Definitions
- Images technique
- Change in belief I
- Change in belief II

Our attitude rests on a set of beliefs that we have in a given situation or about an activity (work – family) or a person.

If you change your beliefs, you change your attitude.

Definition of a belief

A belief is a generalised idea. It is a personal assertion that we believe to be true. It concerns the perception we have of the world, of things in general and of oneself.

Beliefs can be deduced or induced. They have the power to create or to destroy. They are a psychological reality without having a real logic.

Try a little experiment that will show that everything you see is not necessarily real. Stare at a point on the ceiling or at the top of wall. Circle it with your index fingers

Yes! You can see an extra finger, but it's not true. You have 10 fingers not 11.

Your beliefs are the result of the perceptions, deductions, interpretations that (moreover) you have generalised. All individuals builds their beliefs using what they have observed in their entourage, from the people that are important in their lives. The meaning of your identity or of your mission is often defined with regard to the people you use as a reference.

We can distinguish several types of beliefs. Here are some of them.

Personal beliefs linked to ourselves (when our identity takes a knocking)

The beliefs that are linked to us. Failure does not exist. There are only results. If you identify with failure, you feel devastated. Don't take your mistakes as being personality problems. Keep your identity. Get around your result.

Indeed, when someone says something to you that you don't like, look for the positive intention, make a sandwich or immediately think: "that says nothing about me. She or he is speaking about herself or himself". You can check it in this way: in language there is what is called the surface structure and the deep structure.

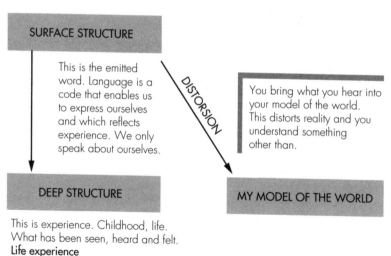

SURFACE STRUCTURE

This is the emitted word. Language is a code that enables us to express ourselves and which reflects experience. We only speak about ourselves.

DISTORSION

You bring what you hear into your model of the world. This distorts reality and you understand something other than.

DEEP STRUCTURE

MY MODEL OF THE WORLD

This is experience. Childhood, life.
What has been seen, heard and felt.
Life experience

100% of people who speak (and you are one of them) have a positive intention. You receive a message that you interpret and obviously you don't understand the intention of the message.

The positive intention of a person who speaks is not necessarily for you, it is for him/her. In the case of parents, if their positive intention concerns you, you can point out that we cannot have an objective for someone else and that they shouldn't worry, you are in control of the situation. In any case, the intention of your interlocutors is not to hurt or to criticise you but to entrust you with their fears, their wishes, their points of view and their beliefs. This never says anything about you. When people speak, they speak only about themselves. Indeed, when you talk to someone, you have an intention and this intention isn't to harm the person but to make her understand something. All too often, however, she will do the same as you and won't understand your intention. She will interpret what you say in her own way.

A father says to his son: "Are you stupid or something?" The child could answer: "No you're not stupid, you don't know how to explain things to me that's all." The surface structure (words) takes us to the deep structure (experience, the VAKOG).

Beliefs reinforced by social proof

Don't rely on what experts say. It isn't because everyone believes something that this thing is true.

Millions of people used to believe the earth was flat and it was even taught in schools. Supposedly the sun turned around the earth because anyone could point a finger at the sky and say: "You see, the sun has moved. So the earth really is the centre of the universe."

In 1543 Copernicus elaborated the first exact representation of our solar system. He had the courage to stand up to all the experts and question what was taught. His theories were accepted after his death.

Permanent beliefs

People who succeed don't believe that a problem will last for the rest of their lives. Pessimists believe that their problem is permanent. This distils a dangerous poison in the body and acts like a computer virus. When you have a cold or a throat infection, you are certain that you'll get over it. Someone who develops a cancer believes it'll be permanent. This is a big problem if you have understood the logical levels and the effect that beliefs have on behaviour. It is much better to believe that any problem is only temporary and that he who says "problem" says "solution."

Global beliefs

If a pessimist doesn't succeed in something or obtains a bad result in one part of his life, everything is ruined. He doesn't see that the family is well or that other things in life are positive. For someone who succeeds, a problem remains a problem. But this doesn't jeopardise the rest. Making a mistake doesn't mean "being a mistake". If you add together permanent belief and global belief the result is terrible.

To succeed in any field, you need to change your limiting or disempowering beliefs and regain the desire to act, to find the useful functions in events, to maintain the sense of your responsibilities and the belief in your personal value.

When you get a virus in your computer, you immediately do what's necessary to get rid of it. It is the same for beliefs that act like viruses on thought. As your unconscious mind is at your service, it becomes a self-fulfilling prophecy.

You should be aware that your beliefs are strictly subjective and I'm going to suggest a few short techniques to help you get rid of them.

Make a list of your beliefs:

- What do I believe about men and women?
- What do I believe about my job?
- What do I believe about myself, about me and my personality?
- What do I believe about my children and my education?
- What do I believe about money?
- Etc.

List all your limiting and disempowering beliefs so you can change them using the following techniques

Images technique

When an image you don't like comes to you and obsesses you, don't ask it to go away because it will come back. The more you refuse it, the more it will return. Accept it, look at it whilst staring at a point in the room or with your eyes closed.

Then push it far, far away. Imagine you are putting the object of your thought on a sledge or on roller skates (your mind will obey you—you are both film producer and operator). Take your time. Then, make the image dark and hazy. When it is far away and you can still vaguely see it, close the curtain.

And now, like magic, make the image of what you want appear in front of you in colour, clear, precise and close to you. Repeat this quickly several times.

Here is an example: a young woman called Sylvie started to develop multiple sclerosis. She kept seeing an image: the image of herself sitting in a wheelchair.

I asked her to take this image, put it on wheels, push it around, backwards, push it away, push it far away, make it dark, hazy and…draw the curtains. Then, like magic, she conjured up an image of Sylvie in front of her. In this image she was standing upright, in a training suit, looking fresh and dynamic. The young woman did this several times until the desired image became automatic. The other image had disappeared for ever and today, by the way, she is cured (and this certainly played a part).

It's easy to do, play with your images.

For your desires: make a clear, precise image of what you want in colour, in 3D and panoramic. Don't see yourself in the image. Act as if you were there and you will feel the emotion of experiencing it.

Perhaps you can add a sound, something you would like to hear.

Create a strong emotion at the idea of getting what you what.

It's as easy as that. The result you get will be amazing…you will get what you imagined.

Change in belief n°1

Hand to hand combat with our questions

- What is preventing me from doing X?
- How do I know this? How do I know I can't?
- What could be the use of the images I'm creating? In what way is it useful for me to believe what I believe?
- What would happen if I started to believe something else, e.g that I am capable of this?
- What would happen if I did what I want to do? (If it's ecological).
- What would happen if I could do it?
- Look for what is true and demonstrable in what you say. You can convince yourself of the absurdity of your limiting beliefs. Decide now to do what you would like to do. Change your belief.

Why should I believe (e.g. that I can't) or believe what I believe?

"What if my belief was wrong? Why should I continue to act and behave as if it was true?"

It's not real facts that disturb you but the belief you have about these facts. Either you've created this belief by yourself, borrowed it from people around you or from people in general.

Get angry with this belief, be furious. When you think about it make an improper gesture. Put your fingers in your nose or stick your tongue out.

Then choose an intense desire, something you really wanted and create emotion. Make a clear and precise image of the expected outcome.

Don't forget that the role of conscious thought is to know what is true and to check that what you are thinking about is really what you want. It's not at all rational to cling to something you don't really want.

Formulate hypotheses, correct evaluations. Reason with the words "when...", "as soon as..." Think of what you have to do as being something easy and entrust your unconscious mind with it. It will happen all by itself.

Simply maintain your pleasant images and emotions.

Change in belief n° 2: the "on the floor with paper" technique

- Choose a limiting or disempowering belief that is bothering you.
- In what context do you believe it? Or, in what type of situation does this belief limit you?
- Write the context of the situation down on a piece of paper, along with what you tell yourself, what you see and put it on the floor.
- Stand opposite the piece of paper. Adopt a thinking stance. Breathe deeply, relax and look at the situation with its belief from a distance.
- Now imagine that the context, the situation comes and surrounds you. You can even call on it to come and surround you.
- What do you need now? What is your intention in this situation? Or, what would you need now? Imagine the solutions and picture the final outcome.

Values

Things you are looking for that will change your life

Love – harmony – success – money – success at work – happy couple – happy family – cleanliness – order – courage – beauty – health – learning – humour – honesty – pride – self-fulfilment – justice – respect – recognition – value – morals – serenity – peace – politeness – and so on.

- **Make a list** of what is important for you. At least 7 values that give a meaning to your life today.
- **Take your values one by one.** We're going to check the belief you have put under them and what your intention is for each value. Check whether your rule depends on other people, whether it is rigid and whether it is spoiling your life. Do as follows:

Here is an example: a student says **"respect"** to me.

LIMITATION

1: What does **respect** mean for you? What needs to happen for you to feel respected?

"That people accept me as I am."

2: Give me a situation in which you didn't feel respected:

"Well, a friend of mine wanted a godmother for her grand-daughter and she didn't know who to choose, she asked me if I was interested. I was really pleased and said to her: "let me know soon, I'm so pleased". I've been waiting for her answer for two months."

3: What was your intention?

"That she should understand me and give me a quick answer."

Can you see the rigid rule?

Her deadline isn't realistic and she's the one who doesn't respect the fact that her friend is undecided or the way she acts.

SUCCESS

Let's keep the intention.

What shall I decide to do to feel respected in everyday life and satisfy my intention?

"I decide to accept people as they are and to respect the way they function, which doesn't prevent me having my own way of doing things. In this case, I respect my friend's indecisiveness and I wait.

I apply my own definition to myself, I accept my friend as she is."

Here is another example with the same value "respect"

LIMITATION	SUCCESS
1: What does **respect** mean for you? "It means accepting what exists, what people are, accepting their ideas." 2: Give me a situation in which you didn't feel respected. "My husband's children (9 and 13) have come to live with us. They don't respect the rules and don't respect me." 3: What was your intention? "That they accept the house rules." **Can you see how she is expecting the environment to fulfil her value?**	**Keeping the intention**, what are you going to decide to do to get respect in everyday life and satisfy your intention? "When the children arrived she never asked them what meal times were like with their mother, what bedtime was like and how this and that used to happen." Not only are their parents no longer together but they have to comply with new rules virtually overnight. 1: I will ask them about their habits. 2: I will respect their tastes and way of doing things. 3: Using the sandwich technique, I will get them to say what would be good for the family. I will respect what they are and their ideas, (I will apply my own rule).

Here is a different person (a man) with the value: "flexibility".

LIMITATION	SUCCESS
1: What does **flexibility** mean for you? What needs to happen for you to feel you are experiencing flexibility? "It's when each person can do what he/she needs to do." 2: Give me an example of a situation where this value wasn't satisfied. "On Sundays, I'd like to have lunch with my partner at 1 p.m. but she prepares the meal for 2 p.m." 3: So what is your intention? "I'd like to have lunch at 1 p.m. and I'd like her to understand that" **Can you see that he's the one who is not flexible? He wants his partner to be. But he's the one who is staking claim to this value.**	**Keeping your intention.** What are you going to decide to do to be flexible? "I'll either accept that it's more convenient for my partner to eat at 2 p.m., or I'll prepare the meal myself for 1 p.m.". Everyone can do what they want and do what they need to do (I apply my own rule).

What are the most important values for you or: what is important for you at work, at home, with the children? Love, consideration, respect, recognition, success, money?

Values	What is my intention?	**Relax your rule.** How can I decide to develop it in on a daily basis, making it flexible for others and easy for me? What behaviour can I adopt? So that it depends only on me!

Your life will change when you are the only source of your own emotions and when your values depend only on you. It will also change when your anti-values have been turned into values.

Here's an example:

What are you afraid of in life or what do you want to avoid? **Mediocrity**	What does mediocrity mean for you? Not succeeding in what we undertake. **You see the rigid rule!** Mistakes are a step on the path to success, hence of learning. The 5th and 6th laws of success. Give yourself realistic deadlines.	What do you do in concrete terms to avoid it? I make a lot of effort, I get stressed. **So much energy wasted!** What was your intention? To succeed in what I'd planned.	Rather than avoiding it, what could you look for? –Patience –Simplicity –Flexibility –Creativity **Replace your anti-values by several easy values**

Summary: values—example: "love" (value by value)

- First question: what does "love" mean for me? What needs to happen for there to be love in my life?
- Second question: I look for an example, a situation where it didn't happen: what was my intention? (write it down on a piece of paper)
- Third question: respecting this intention, what am I going to do in concrete terms to develop love on a daily basis and satisfy my intention, that depends only on me? **This value belongs to me.**

Summary: Anti-values:

- What do I want to avoid? What am I afraid of? (e.g: nastiness, meanness)
- What does nastiness mean for me? How, in concrete terms, do I avoid it on a daily basis? I find a precise situation where I wanted to avoid it.
- What was my intention?
- Rather than avoiding it, what could I look for?

Put 3 or 4 values to replace each anti-value.

Well done! You are taking control of your emotions and your destiny.

An anchor

What is anchoring?

It is a trigger that sparks off an emotion. A stimulus/response.

Something, an image, a sound, triggers a reaction in you and you are not necessarily aware of this.

For example, you go shopping in a supermarket, you hear a piece of music, this music reminds you that you danced with X two years ago. This is an auditory anchor.

A wink or a smile are visual anchors.

A thought can trigger an emotion instantly.

An emotion is attached to a situation and the creators of Neuro-Linguistic Programming (NLP) thought it would be great to anchor the emotions we would need in a particular situation.

- Select the emotion, the resource you would need
- Connect it
- Use it as needed

When you want to leave someone you have loved very much the most difficult things to give up are the anchors. Even when you know it is best to leave, you cling to the memory of all the anchors: visual, auditory, kinesthetic. It's a bit like tying a knot in clothes before washing them. And, as the French comedian Coluche, a French humorist, said: "then try undoing the knot!" It's the same for anchors. Deactivating them is specialist's work.

Resource anchoring

1. Look for the Situation. In which situation or context do you need something extra, a helpful resource? (e.g. a useful and appropriate emotion). For example: "asking my boss for a rise", or "sitting an exam".

2. Resource – In this situation, in this context, which emotion, which feeling, which inner state would be ideal? (being dynamic, pleased, happy, motivated, convincing, positive, reassuring, self-confident, etc). For example, "self confident".

3. Go back into your near or distant past and search in your memory for a time in your life when had this feeling, this emotion. In this example: "being self-confident".

4. When you have found it, close your eyes or stare at a point in the room. Relive this scene in your imagination, relive the exact moment when you felt this emotion. In the example: "the moment you felt self confident".

5. Check that you cannot see yourself in the picture. Act as if you were there. You can see everything around you. When you find the emotion you are looking for, when you get the feeling as strongly as you can, clench your fist. Your clenched fist will be your anchor.

6. Then open your eyes and your fist. After a few moments, clench your fist again to check that you feel the emotion when you clench it.

7. Now imagine the future and in your imagination go into the situation in which you needed this resource and experience the context as best you can with a new, resourceful attitude.

When you clench your fist, you will reactivate this anchor, only for the situation you have chosen. You won't be able to anchor a permanent state for all situations.

Behaviour Generator

All behaviour can be useful in a certain context, but not in all contexts. People who succeed have the ability to change their behaviour by naturally adapting to situations. As contexts change, the same behaviour will not necessarily produce the same result.

Telling a dirty story in a sports meeting may be funny but the same story told during the meal after a communion won't go down well. Talking to your boss in the same baby's voice you use to talk to your child would sound ridiculous.

It is therefore essential to remember that no behaviour has any meaning outside the context in which it was generated.

Change your behaviours

The meaning of communication is the response it gets.

It is our responsibility to make ourselves understood and the response we get is the result of the behaviour we have set up. This means we are responsible for the reaction of others. When someone gets angry with you, shouts at you, this is in response to what you have just done. Yes, I know. This isn't what you thought.

Change your behaviour (your way of speaking too) and you will change the environment.

Self esteem and behaviour

Have you ever noticed that shy people do exactly the right things to make other people think they are useless? And this is precisely what they don't want, i.e. that people think they're stupid. As the fear of the thing creates the thing, they obtain the dreaded result; people think they are idiots.

Now answer the following question that we touched on in the chapter on Communication.

"What do I want people to think of me when they look at me? What would I like people to believe about me?"

You can ask yourself these questions for different situations. If your answer is: "I don't know", then people won't know what to think of you. If your answer is: "I wouldn't like people to think that I am such and such." This is exactly what people will think.

Now, if in your mind you decide what you want people to think about you: "that you are friendly, sociable, happy, helpful, nice", and if you say these words to yourself in your head, your unconscious mind will provide you with the external behaviour that matches your thoughts.

So, put the words you want into your mind and change your behaviour.

Pascal said: "kneel down, pray and you will believe".

Remember to be congruent[1]. Wanting want people around you to think you know everything, that you are very intelligent and that you understand everything very quickly, is very hard and you may well develop a lack of self confidence. Be simple and congruent.

How to change an unpleasant behaviour

1. In which context or situation would you like to change your behaviour?

2. Put six pieces of paper on the floor (let's imagine you're called Sophie).

---

1 **Being congruent** means adopting the behaviour and attitude that correspond to what I am : saying what I know, what I think, what I believe.

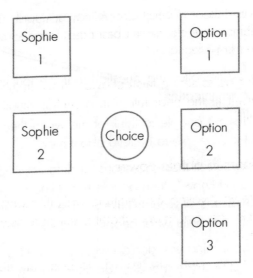

3. I stand on "Sophie 1", I speak about my problem in this situation and I adopt the behaviour I don't like in this problem.

"What is my intention in this situation when I adopt this behaviour? What do I want? What do I believe?"

4. I move to "Sophie 2", I breathe deeply, I adopt the behaviour of someone who is thinking and I look at Sophie 1.

I ask myself: "What would "Sophie 1" need to satisfy her intention? What else could she believe that would be more useful in this situation or this context? Maybe she could set up other behaviours and other choices".

5. I choose 3 solutions, 3 options or possibilities, i.e. 3 new behaviours that would respect the initial intention and which would be more appropriate in this context. I can also choose a more useful belief.

I write my solutions on 3 pieces of paper and go and place each of them respectively on the 3 options squares.

I then go from Option 1 to Option 2 and to Option 3 to live and experience these 3 solutions. (So, I go respectively from one paper to another, from one option to another) and I as certain that each option would be useful and appropriate in the context.

6. I then move onto the paper called "Choice" (the central piece of paper I put on the floor). I close my eyes and I spin around several times. I open my eyes again, a little dizzy, I stagger a little in one

direction and I look at which option I am facing. My unconscious mind will make me choose the best possible solution, one of the three, the most adequate.

You can decide to set up this behaviour now, in this context and imagine yourself in the near future in a similar situation with your new personality.

Four behaviours to obtain power

When we are very young we begin to walk (9 months to 1 year). We very quickly become aware that it is our parents who have the power and not us.

"Don't touch this, don't do that, go to bed, say hello, put your toys away…" This soon becomes unbearable and 100% of people want power. We will very quickly set up behaviours (unconsciously) to draw on other people's energy and thereby get power.

1 — *The interrogators*

These people are always asking questions. The interrogators start as soon as they can talk. "What's this? Where's that? Why this? Why that?" It's exhausting. When they become adults they continue. They take a great deal of interest in you and ask lots of questions about you and your life. They are very friendly, parental, easy-going but they criticise everything you do. That's not the way to do it. They always know better than you. Their way of doing things is the best.

A man with an interrogating wife puts a glass down somewhere but not where he should have put it. He wants to wash the dishes: "that's not how you dry dishes!" she says. So, he stops doing anything. Of course, as far as the interrogating mother in law is concerned, this type of thing can turn into "bitter attacks".

2 — *The complainers*

As children they were always crying. They were supported when they came up against older kids; they were the winners. They were given kisses and sweets. It works!! They suck out your energy and attract your attention.

As adults: there is always something wrong with them. Always complaining about something and you can never do enough for them. It's never their fault. When they are ill they have to moan. Plaintive women cry a lot and this works very well at the beginning of a marriage but not long term.

3 — The indifferent

We never know what's going on. They hide away in their room and don't speak. This obviously exhausts the mother who starts asking herself existential questions. If she's a complainer she'll cry. If she's an interrogator she'll feel very ill at ease with her unanswered questions.

"Say something darling. What's the matter honey?" These are very bad tactics.

Indifferent people suck out other people's energy by remaining silent and indefinable. Let them get on with it. Simply say: "hey, Mister indifferent" and wait for them to come back. Men need to return to their caves. Leave them to it. When they come out they will be more amorous than ever.

4 — The intimidators

They speak loudly, shout a lot. This can go as far as blackmail, they yell.

Speaking loudly doesn't mean being right. It means that this is the only way they can get people to listen to them. It is the only way they can intimidate. Intimidators also draw on your energy, they insist on what they are saying to convince you. This can work with weak people or people in an external frame of reference.

Have fun trying to identify what you do and giving a name to your behaviour. You can draw energy from the universe by observing the beauty of a tree and by putting your arms around it. Look at the flowers and mentally speak to them, telling them they're beautiful.

People often have these 4 behaviours in the same day, sometimes within an hour. When one doesn't work they go onto another (unconsciously, of course).

If you are the child of an interrogator, you have become a complainer or indifferent, which is no better. You make everyone around you feel guilty.

In the street you can see a lot of young people who have become intimidators. Their father was one but they couldn't answer back at home, otherwise they would've been slapped. So they make up for it outside to obtain power.

It's better to be aware of this and realise that wanting power is useless. Learning to communicate and accepting others is much more pleasant because you stay young and in good health much longer.

Determining an objective – Summary

How do we reach an objective? This is the logical reasoning of your brain.

If I go through the steps below, I can reach my objective.

Before that I must know:

1. What is the point in reaching my objective?

   If my unconscious mind doesn't see the point, I can't do anything. What would it bring me that I don't have today?

2. Not to fear losing something by reaching my objective.

   What would frighten me? Finding solutions.

What is my **present state?**		What is my **desired state?**
What is my life today?		What I want instead
I will spend 10% of my time on the problem	⇨	I spend 90% of my time on the solutions

I then check 4 important points. This is a **PREM**.

The objective can only be PERSONAL. I cannot reach an objective for someone else. I cannot want anything for my husband or children. Each person must desire something for himself. The objective can concern a group and in this case everyone should be in agreement.

My objective will be:

Precise
- I know what I want. I know to what end. My intention is to do so and so.
- I know what this will bring me and in what way it is important for me
- I can define what I want, I am able to visualise it.

Realistic – Responsible (internal frame of reference)
- It is realistic for me. I know how to go about it in practical terms.
- I'm the one who wants it. I'm the one who decides. I do everything for that…
- I'm getting everything moving so I can do X…

Ecological
- I check it's in my best interests.
- All the parts of me agree. I am entirely in agreement with that. There are no drawbacks for my environment.

Measurable
- I fix myself a realistic time limit of X. In 6 months or one year, to this day, I will reach this goal.
- How will I know I have made the right choice? I will know when…

Criteria to determine an objective for change

Here are the characteristics to check for a precise, realistic, ecological and measurable objective:

Precise
- Clear, affirmatively formulated, contextualised. I look for the intention of the intention.
- I can define it, visualise it (clear, close and precise image in colour)

Realistic
- Reachable, given the context.
- Only depends on myself – **responsible**.

Ecological

- Do all the parts of me agree? For a group objective, all the parties need to agree.
- Good for me and good for others.
- It respects or restores the balance with your inner self and with other people.
- Takes into account the advantages of the present state (especially the secondary benefits). There are always positive aspects in your present state. Learn to preserve them (often intentions).

Measurable

- Personal accomplishment criteria – realistic deadlines

Perception, an automatic phenomenon

The perception you have of yourself and others is a purely natural and automatic phenomenon that has been passed on to you by your family. The way in which you perceive people around you and even you own body, determines the world in which you live. If you change your perception, you change your world (the belief, the idea changes the environment). In fact, the environment doesn't change. It behaves in accordance with your expectations.

Everything depends on the attitude you have in the face of life and events. If you adopt an inquisitive, positive, loving, audacious and tolerant attitude, the world in which you live will begin to look like you would like it to be.

As the map is not the territory, each individual seems independent whereas in fact we are all connected to levels of intelligence that govern the whole of the cosmos. Our spirit is an aspect of a universal spirit and we are never alone. If you put your entire trust in this process, the answers to your questions and requests will reach you via a much vaster intelligence than your conscious spirit. Be trusting. Give things the time they need to happen. When you have a problem or a desire, entrust your energy with it.

Energy will answer your expectations. The information will always reach you and be totally relevant. Information is a permanent flow that we consciously filter according to our needs. Just like the "bold type" key on the computer keyboard, your will selects what you need to know.

As you get closer to an upper level of vibration, the messages obviously arrive more quickly.

When you use your talents and capabilities with a positive or beneficial intention, things will come to you.

If you don't feel this flow, change your objectives until they show you a way back to your path.

Expect, in one day, to meet people who have useful messages concerning your actions or your thoughts (see chapter on "Synchronicities").

If you sharpen your awareness to this phenomenon, it will happen.

If you sharpen your awareness to doubt, to scepticism, to other people's expectations, then either nothing will happen or the opposite will happen.

When you want to transfer positive energy, it is impossible for you to fail because in the field of subtle interaction, **wanting means acting**.

The necessary condition for success to exist is the awareness that success is within your reach.

You can change your mental strategies and radically change your behaviours

The VAKOG

- **V**isual
- **A**uditive
- **K**inesthetic
- **O**lfactory
- **G**ustative

A mental strategy is an internal and unconscious process that you set up to pass from the present state to the desired state.

This can be observed with a person's eye movement and the words she uses.

e.g. A young woman says to me: "I'm always late, I'd like to be on time." I ask her: "In your opinion, how do you manage to be late?" Her answer: "I can't get out of bed."

Let's look at the strategy she uses to "not get up".

First of all, I tell her about my own strategy because it's no problem for me to get up as soon as the alarm clock rings

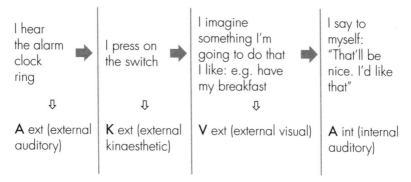

I hear the alarm clock ring	I press on the switch	I imagine something I'm going to do that I like: e.g. have my breakfast	I say to myself: "That'll be nice. I'd like that"
A ext (external auditory)	**K** ext (external kinaesthetic)	**V** ext (external visual)	**A** int (internal auditory)

And I get up. So here is my strategy:

A external → K external → V external → A internal → I get up

Now here is this young woman's strategy:

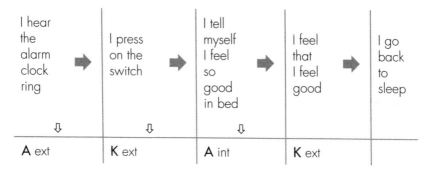

I hear the alarm clock ring	I press on the switch	I tell myself I feel so good in bed	I feel that I feel good	I go back to sleep
A ext	**K** ext	**A** int	**K** ext	

The beginning is identical and the end of her strategy is perfect for going back to sleep.

Here's what we change. As soon as she's heard the alarm clock and pressed the switch, we replace her internal **A** and her internal

K by the image of meeting the love of her life in the underground station = internal **V**. Now she gets up as soon as the alarm rings but she has also met the love of her life, which is quite a feat.

Have fun studying (in slow motion) the way in which you do something. One action leads to another. Ask yourself the question each time: "Immediately after, what do I do?"

For example, a child says: "I can't manage to do my homework when I go home."

"As soon as you're home, what do you *do?*

I have a snack.	= **G** external
I see the mess on my desk.	= **V**isual external
I have an image of the TV in my head.	= **V**isual internal
What can he do?	
He goes home and has a snack.	= **G** external.
He sits down at his desk.	= **K** external(replaced).
He looks at his diary.	= **V** external (replaced).
He imagines the teacher giving him a good mark.	= **V** internal.

Sometimes it is enough to change one parameter to see one behaviour disappear and be replaced by another.

Here is another learning strategy:

V external	V external	A internal	V internal	K	A internal
I look at my class notebook	I skim over it quickly, reading diagonally	I repeat to myself the words I have just read	I make an internal, visual representation of it for myself.	I feel good	I repeat to myself what I have just read, to check

The Seven laws of success according to Herbert Armstrong

There are laws in the universe and man has come into the world to succeed. You didn't come here to be poor, ill, ugly, etc. Man has received orders to evolve and succeed.

How do we arrive at this goal? It is very important to be aware of these laws to succeed in life. They are complementary to what you have learned about determining objectives.

- **First law:** fix yourself "PREM" objectives and make them a focal point of your life, the underlying motivation.
- **Second law:** education, preparation. Aim to be competent in what you do. Set yourself realistic deadlines. Far too many people today neglect this essential second law of knowledge and learning. Understanding is one thing, knowing how to do something is another.
- **Third law:** being in good health. Your body must be in good shape: you can have intelligent and subtle thoughts but everything is spoiled if you're not in good health. A healthy body means a healthy personality. The potential to use our thought, our vital energy (breathing, eating habits, adequate thoughts).
- **Fourth law:** law of action.
  Having initiative. With a healthy body we set in motion the energy inside us and we go into action. We must decide to pass from the abstract to the concrete.
- **Fifth law:** resourcefulness.
  This is a fundamental law. Hence, there is no failure, only results or feedback. You will always come up against unexpected events. You need to be resourceful and capable of reacting. Be flexible.
  "If things don't go as planned, learn to adapt, to get around things, to act a little differently. Study your result or do something else."
- **Sixth law:** perseverance.
  This means constant repetition so that results appear much later on. It is just when things are getting hard and when you persevere that you reach your goal. Never moan. Stay positive and keep your eye on the target.

With these 6 laws, success is already yours along with everything you need. But sometimes you may experience an inner emptiness that goes with this success. A seventh law will complete your work. This depends on people and on the changes in which you find yourself.

- **Seventh law:** spirituality.

  Communication with the ultimate principle. Relationship with the universe and superior plans.

  You don't need this law to succeed materially, but this 7th law brings you achievement, the intimate conviction of a job well done, serenity. Being where you belong in the universe and respecting your principles, as I explained in the chapter on Abundance.

How to get rid of a negative thought

When a negative thought comes to mind – Technique 1

- I imagine I can see myself and I put the thought in front of me (if necessary in a bubble)
- I look at myself, with the thought above my head (use your first name: I can see Juliette)
- I place myself above the thought.
- I look at it and say to myself: "Look now, this mind is having a thought and this body is having a feeling".
- I have thoughts but I am not my thoughts and I don't have to listen to what my thoughts are saying to me.

To get rid of a negative thought – Technique 2

The brain obeys laws. There are 5 of them.

If your thought fits into 3 of these laws, keep it.

If your thought doesn't fit into 3 of these laws, it is bad for you and you must change it. You don't need to do anything, your brain will take care of it by itself.

Write the 5 questions below on a piece of paper.

- Get comfortable in an armchair.
- Take this piece of paper in your hands and answer "yes" or "no" to these questions. Above all, no sentences.

When you've finished, you will notice that the thought has disappeared. Put your thought the place of X.

1. Is my thought (X) based on real or objective facts?
2. Will the fact of acting on this thought (X) (or emotion) help me protect my life or my health?
3. Will thinking in this way (X) help me reach my short term or long term goals?
4. Will thinking in this way (X) best help me avoid the most unwanted conflicts with others?
5. Will thinking in this way (X) enable me to feel what I'd like to feel if I was feeling good in myself? (no cigarettes or medicines)

Go back to what you were doing and let your unconscious mind go to work.

You can change everything...now!

Achevé d'imprimer en France par Présence Graphique
2, rue de la Pinsonnière - 37260 Monts
N° d'imprimeur : 101140062

Dépôt légal : octobre 2011